EXTENDED ESSAY WORKBOOK

Name of the Student:

Grade:

IB Candidate number:

School:

Session: May 2026

Pranab Sharma,
FRSA

ISBN 979-8-89699-490-9

Definition and Purpose

The IB extended essay is part of the core requirements/curriculum of an IB Diploma Program and involves focused independent research by the IB student on a chosen theme. Resulting papers have a typical length of up to 4000 words long (they should tend to reach this, although writing 3500 words can still be acceptable). A low score (E) for the extended paper and/or Theory of Knowledge essay revokes the right to receive an IB Diploma. By contrast, good marks contribute to the overall score, which could impact a student's college application success.

While submission deadlines for extended essays are set by the IB, schools are free to set their own internal deadlines. Preparation and work on this assignment spans several academic terms – this includes choosing extended essay topics, submitting proposals, designating supervisors, information gathering (e.g. sources from local libraries), writing a draft (for instance, over a summer break), receiving feedback from supervisors, etc.

Pranab Sharma

FRSA, IBDP Extended Essay Examiner

WHAT IS THE EXTENDED ESSAY?

The Extended Essay (EE) is a compulsory, externally assessed piece of independent research into a topic chosen by the student and presented as a formal piece of academic writing. The extended essay is intended to promote high-level research and writing skills, intellectual discovery and creativity while engaging students in personal research. This leads to a major piece of formally presented, structured writing of up to 4,000 words in which ideas and findings are communicated in a reasoned, coherent and appropriate manner.

Students are guided through the process of research and writing by an assigned supervisor (a teacher in the school). All students undertake three mandatory reflection sessions with their supervisor, including a short interview, or viva voce, following the completion of the extended essay.

Extended Essay (EE) topics may be chosen from a list of approved DP subjects—normally one of the student's six chosen subjects for the IB diploma or the world studies option. World Studies (WS) provides students with the opportunity to carry out an in-depth interdisciplinary study of an issue of contemporary global significance, using two IB disciplines.

The aims of the EE are to provide students with the opportunity to:

- engage in independent research with intellectual initiative and rigour
- develop research, thinking, self- management and communication skills
- reflect on what has been learned throughout the research and writing process

The EE, including the World Studies option, is assessed against common criteria and is interpreted in ways appropriate to each subject.

Students are expected to:

- provide a logical and coherent rationale for their choice of topic
- review what has already been written about the topic
- formulate a clear research question
- offer a concrete description of the methods used to investigate the question
- generate reasoned interpretations and conclusions based on their reading and independent research in order to answer the question
- reflect on what has been learned throughout the research and writing process.

The EE contributes to the student's overall score for the Diploma through the award of points in conjunction with Theory of Knowledge. A maximum of three points are awarded according to a student's combined performance in both the Extended Essay and Theory of Knowledge.

ASSESSMENT CRITERIA

Criterion A: Focus and Method

This criterion focuses on the topic, the research question and the methodology. It assesses the explanation of the focus of the research (this includes the topic and the research question), how the research will be undertaken, and how the focus is maintained throughout the essay.

LEVEL	DESCRIPTOR OF STRANDS AND INDICATORS
0	The work does not reach a standard outlined by the descriptors below.
1-2	**The topic is communicated unclearly and incompletely.** • Identification and explanation of the topic is limited; the purpose and focus of the research is unclear, or does not lend itself to a systematic investigation in the subject for which it is registered. **The research question is stated but not clearly expressed or too broad** • The research question is too broad in scope to be treated effectively within the word limit and requirements of the task, or does not lend itself to a systematic investigation in the subject for which it is registered. • The intent of the research question is understood but has not been clearly expressed and/or the discussion of the essay is not focused on the research question. **Methodology of the research is limited.** • The source(s) and/or method(s) to be used are limited in range given the topic and research question. • There is limited evidence that their selection was informed.
3-4	**The topic is communicated.** • Identification and explanation of the research topic is communicated; the purpose and focus of the research is adequately clear, but only partially appropriate. **The research question is clearly stated but only partially focused.** • The research question is clear but the discussion in the essay is only partially focused and connected to the research question. **Methodology of the research is mostly complete.** • Source(s) and/or method(s) to be used are generally relevant and appropriate given the topic and research question. • There is some evidence that their selection(s) was informed. **If the topic or research question is deemed inappropriate for the subject in which the essay is registered no more than four marks can be awarded for this criterion.**
5-6	**The topic is communicated accurately and effectively.** • Identification and explanation of the research topic is effectively communicated; the purpose and focus of the research is clear and appropriate. **The research question is clearly stated and focused.** • The research question is clear and addresses an issue of research that is appropriately connected to the discussion in the essay. **Methodology of the research is complete.** • An appropriate range of relevant source(s) and/or method(s) has been selected in relation to the topic and research question. • There is evidence of effective and informed selection of sources and/or methods.

ASSESSMENT CRITERIA

Criterion B: Knowledge and Understanding

This criterion assesses the extent to which the research relates to the subject area/discipline used to explore the research question, or in the case of the world studies extended essay, the issue addressed and the two disciplinary perspectives applied, and additionally the way in which this knowledge and understanding is demonstrated through the use of appropriate terminology and concepts.

LEVEL	DESCRIPTOR OF STRANDS AND INDICATORS
0	The work does not reach a standard outlined by the descriptors below.
1-2	**Knowledge and understanding is limited.** • The application of source material has limited relevance and is only partially appropriate to the research question. • Knowledge of the topic/discipline(s)/issue is anecdotal, unstructured and mostly descriptive with sources not effectively being used. **Use of terminology and concepts is unclear and limited.** • Subject-specific terminology and/or concepts are either missing or inaccurate, demonstrating limited knowledge and understanding.
3-4	**Knowledge and understanding is good.** • The application of source material is mostly relevant and appropriate to the research question. • Knowledge of the topic/discipline(s)/issue is clear; there is an understanding of the sources used but their application is only partially effective. **Use of terminology and concepts is adequate.** • The use of subject-specific terminology and concepts is mostly accurate, demonstrating an appropriate level of knowledge and understanding. **If the topic or research question is deemed inappropriate for the subject in which the essay is registered no more than four marks can be awarded for this criterion.**
5-6	**Knowledge and understanding is excellent.** • The application of source materials is clearly relevant and appropriate to the research question. • Knowledge of the topic/discipline(s)/issue is clear and coherent and sources are used effectively and with understanding. **Use of terminology and concepts is good.** • The use of subject-specific terminology and concepts is accurate and consistent, demonstrating effective knowledge and understanding.

ASSESSMENT CRITERIA

Criterion C: Critical Thinking

This criterion assesses the extent to which critical-thinking skills have been used to analyse and evaluate the research undertaken.

LEVEL	DESCRIPTOR OF STRANDS AND INDICATORS
0	The work does not reach a standard outlined by the descriptors below.
1-3	**The research is limited.** • The research presented is limited and its application to support the argument is not clearly relevant to the research question. **Analysis is limited.** • There is limited analysis. • Where there are conclusions to individual points of analysis these are limited and not consistent with the evidence. **Discussion/evaluation is limited.** • An argument is outlined but this is limited, incomplete, descriptive or narrative in nature. The construction of an argument is unclear and/or incoherent in structure hindering understanding. • Where there is a final conclusion, it is limited and not consistent with the arguments/evidence presented. • There is an attempt to evaluate the research, but this is superficial. **If the topic or research question is deemed inappropriate for the subject in which the essay is registered no more than three marks can be awarded for this criterion.**
4-6	**The research is adequate.** • Some research presented is appropriate and its application to support the argument is partially relevant to the research question. **Analysis is adequate.** • There is analysis but this is only partially relevant to the research question; the inclusion of irrelevant research detracts from the quality of the argument. • Any conclusions to individual points of analysis are only partially supported by the evidence. **Discussion/evaluation is adequate.** • An argument explains the research but the reasoning contains inconsistencies. The argument may lack clarity and coherence but this does not significantly hinder understanding. • Where there is a final or summative conclusion, this is only partially consistent with the arguments/evidence presented. • The research has been evaluated but not critically.

LEVEL	DESCRIPTOR OF STRANDS AND INDICATORS
7-9	**The research is good.** • The majority of the research is appropriate and its application to support the argument is clearly relevant to the research question. **Analysis is good.** • The research is analysed in a way that is clearly relevant to the research question; the inclusion of less relevant research rarely detracts from the quality of the overall analysis. Conclusions to individual points of analysis are supported by the evidence but there are some minor inconsistencies. **Discussion/evaluation is good.** • An effective reasoned argument is developed from the research, with a conclusion supported by the evidence presented. • This reasoned argument is clearly structured and coherent and supported by a final or summative conclusion; minor inconsistencies may hinder the strength of the overall argument. • The research has been evaluated, and this is partially critical.
10-12	**The research is excellent.** • The research is appropriate to the research question and its application to support the argument is consistently relevant. **Analysis is excellent.** • The research is analysed effectively and clearly focused on the research question; the inclusion of less relevant research does not significantly detract from the quality of the overall analysis. • Conclusions to individual points of analysis are effectively supported by the evidence. **Discussion/evaluation is excellent.** • An effective and focused reasoned argument is developed from the research with a conclusion reflective of the evidence presented. • This reasoned argument is well structured and coherent; any minor inconsistencies do not hinder the strength of the overall argument or the final or summative conclusion. • The research has been critically evaluated.

ASSESSMENT CRITERIA

Criterion D: Presentation

This criterion assesses the extent to which critical-thinking skills have been used to analyse and evaluate the research undertaken.

LEVEL	DESCRIPTOR OF STRANDS AND INDICATORS
0	The work does not reach a standard outlined by the descriptors below.
1-2	**Presentation is acceptable.** • The structure of the essay is generally appropriate in terms of the expected conventions for the topic, argument and subject in which the essay is registered. Some layout considerations may be missing or applied incorrectly. • Weaknesses in the structure and/or layout do not significantly impact the reading, understanding or evaluation of the extended essay.
3-4	**Presentation is good.** • The structure of the essay clearly is appropriate in terms of the expected conventions for the topic, the argument and subject in which the essay is registered. • Layout considerations are present and applied correctly. • The structure and layout support the reading, understanding and evaluation of the extended essay.

ASSESSMENT CRITERIA

Criterion E: Engagement

This criterion assesses the student's engagement with their research focus and the research process. It will be applied by the examiner at the end of the assessment of the essay, and is based solely on the candidate's reflections as detailed on the RPPF, with the supervisory comments and extended essay itself as context. Only the first 500 words are assessable.

LEVEL	DESCRIPTOR OF STRANDS AND INDICATORS
0	The work does not reach a standard outlined by the descriptors, an RPPF has not been submitted, or the RPPF has been submitted in a language other than that of the essay.
1-2	**Engagement is limited.** • Reflections on decision-making and planning are mostly descriptive. • These reflections communicate a limited degree of personal engagement with the research focus and/or research process.
3-4	**Engagement is good.** • Reflections on decision-making and planning are analytical and include reference to conceptual understanding and skill development. • These reflections communicate a moderate degree of personal engagement with the research focus and process of research, demonstrating some intellectual initiative.
5-6	**Engagement is excellent.** • Reflections on decision-making and planning are evaluative and include reference to the student's capacity to consider actions and ideas in response to challenges experienced in the research process. • These reflections communicate a high degree of intellectual and personal engagement with the research focus and process of research, demonstrating authenticity, intellectual initiative and/or creative approach in the student voice.

Overview

Criterion A: focus and method	Criterion B: knowledge and understanding	Criterion C: critical thinking	Criterion D: presentation	Criterion E: engagement
• Topic • Research question • Methodology	• Context • Subject-specific terminology and concepts	• Research • Analysis • Discussion and evaluation	• Structure • Layout	• Process • Research focus
Marks	Marks	Marks	Marks	Marks
6	6	12	4	6

Total marks available: 34

Assessment Criteria decoded for the first draft

Criterion A: Focus and Method

Worth = 6 marks

To access these marks you need to ensure that you clearly state your:

1. subject and topic
2. RQ (Research Question)
3. methods, major source, and range of sources investigated
4. range of sources is appropriate and determined by the subject area (primary, secondary, experiments). This can be checked on your **Subject Reports**
5. justification for carrying out this research (Why is this topic worthy of investigation?)

Criterion B: Knowledge and Understanding

Worth = 6 marks

To access these marks you need to ensure that you clearly:

1. set up the context of your research within your selected subject area
2. you apply subject specific terminology and concepts
3. resources are supported by effectively using subject area terminology and concepts

Criterion C: Critical Thinking

Worth = 12 marks

To access these marks you need to ensure that your:

1. research is consistent and relevant to the subject area
2. sources are used appropriately to demonstrate depth of understanding
3. discussions in essay demonstrate individual command of terminology, concepts, and analysis
4. analysis is focused on your RQ
5. arguments or conclusions you state are supported with evidence (here use things like The 5 W's or OPVL to solidify your findings)
6. arguments and conclusions are well structured and coherently explained

Criterion D: Presentation

Worth = AN EASY 4 marks

To access these marks you need to ensure that your:

1. Title Page is correct
2. Introduction has the following:
   - RQ
   - Focus of essay
   - Scope of research
   - Indication of sources to be used
   - Insights into the argument to be made
   - Why the topic is important to the subject area
3. Headers are consistent and logical (Introduction, Body, Conclusions, etc)
4. Conclusion addresses the original RQ
5. Works Cited is alphabetical
6. Citations are in MLA Format and INCLUDE: standard information, PLUS: Web Addresses, Date Accessed (IB Mandate)
7. Images, graphs, charts, and tables are properly located and identified (ie. in the Appendices)
8. Essay has page numbers

Criterion E: Engagement

Worth = 6 marks

To access these marks you need to ensure that your reflections:

1. Talk about decisions you made during the research process
2. Changes, difficulties, or alternative thinking you had as you worked through the essay
3. Supports you need or wanted throughout the process
4. Are no more than 500 words total
5. Are delivered (Uploaded) on time

THE RESEARCHER'S REFLECTION SPACE (RRS)

Student reflection in the Extended Essay is critical. Effective reflection highlights the engagement of the student in an intellectual and personal process and how this has changed the student as a learner and affected the completion of that individual's essay.

For those students who have completed the Middle Years Programme, the researcher's reflection space (RRS) can be compared to the process journal. The IB considers this to be a central component of a successful research process as it:

- supports student learning, thinking and critical analysis throughout the research process
- helps to stimulate discussions between the student and supervisor
- aids the reflection process.

Use your Researcher's Reflection Space to...

record emerging questions.

create mind maps

record your reflections

respond to artefacts, such as photos, newspaper clippings, twitter feeds, blogs, and so on

collate and reflect on sources

respond to prompts and questions that may arise in the your subject areas, TOK classes or other aspects of the Diploma Programme

make notes on meetings with your supervisor

track and record the progress of your research

MY RR SPACE

MY RRS

MY RRS

As part of the reflection process, you will hold 3 formal reflection meetings with your supervisor. You will then write up your reflections on the *Researcher's Planning and Progress Form* (RPPF). This should total no more than 500 words and is where you will be marked for Criterion E.

"the IB considers the development of the RRS an essential element of good reflective practice as it will help the student to not only scaffold the extended essay process but also to build skills which transcend the task itself and prepare the student for university study and beyond.

A well-used RRS will aid the reflection sessions students have with their supervisor, as elements of it can be used to stimulate and inform discussion. This will help students to move towards a more evaluative understanding of the research process and the choices they make as part of this."

- International Baccalaureate Extended Essay Guide: Supporting the Extended Essay

SESSION 1: FIRST REFLECTION	Students are encouraged to includeexamples of initial topic exploration, possible sources and methods, preliminary research questions and their personal reactions to the issues. In attending their first reflection session with their supervisor, students can use notes made in the RRS as the basis for discussion as well as to demonstrate the progress students have made in the research process.
SESSION 2: INTERIM REFLECTION	Students can demonstrate the progress of their thinking, the development of their argument and raise any questions they may have with their supervisor. At this stage the RRS may include reactions to readings, progress in the timeline for completion of the extended essay, a possible outline of arguments, challenges encountered and the strategies used to overcome them.
SESSION 3: VIVA VOCE	Students can show what they have learned about the topic, the research process followed, their own learning, as well as outlining new questions they have uncovered. Most importantly, during the viva voce the RRS may help to highlight the personal significance of the work to the student and ultimately contribute to the supervisor's report.

QUESTIONS YOU MAY WANT TO ASK YOURSELF WHILST REFLECTING:

- What is going well and why?
- What problems are you encountering and why?
- How have you overcome these problems?
- What decisions have you made and why?
- How has your supervisor supported you?
- What are your next steps and why?
- What is missing and what will you do about it?
- If you could do something again, what would you do and why

Notice the focus on 'why'.

Make sure you are not just describing the process but that you analyse and evaluate it, too.

YOUR SUPERVISOR

Once you have chosen your topic, you will be assigned a supervisor. This is a member of staff within the school and, where possible, will be a subject specialist in your chosen area. If they are not a subject specialist, you may also have a 'mentor' who knows the subject well and can provide additional support. This mentor does not have to be someone who works in the school.

Which words belong to which column? Be prepared to explain your answers.

STUDENT	SUPERVISOR

What other words could you add to these lists?

Encourage **Facilitate** **Comment**

Guide **Write** **Upload**

Monitor **Decide** **Plan**

Research **Help** **Edit**

Support **Organise** **Assess**

ATL SKILLS

> "The development of skills such as thinking skills and communication skills is frequently identified as a crucial element in preparing students effectively for life beyond school. It is also about developing affective and metacognitive skills, and about encouraging students to view learning as something that they "do for themselves in a proactive way, rather than as a covert event that happens to them in reaction to teaching" (Zimmerman 2000: 65).

The term "skill" is used in a broad sense in the DP to encompass cognitive, metacognitive and affective skills. Cognitive skills include all the information processing and thinking skills often called "study skills" in a school environment. Affective skills are the skills of behaviour and emotional management underpinning attitudinal factors like resilience, perseverance and self-motivation, which can often have a large role to play in educational achievement. Metacognitive skills are the skills that students can use to monitor the effectiveness of their learning skills and processes, to better understand and evaluate their learning.

Although these skills may be in use when manifesting a certain natural ability or talent, they are different to both of these because proficiency in any skill can be increased through the deliberate use of techniques and strategies, feedback and challenge. Skills are therefore highly teachable."

- International Baccalaureate: Programme Standards and Practices

- Mind map what these skills mean and what they might look like.
- How can you use the EE process to develop them?
- Where and how are they assessed throughout the process?

Be sure to reflect on the development of these in your RSS and RPPF

Response

GETTING THE EXTENDED ESSAY STARTED

Five steps to developing an RQ

1.Choose a subject and topic that is of interest.

Deciding on a subject and topic that is of interest and in which the student is personally invested is important if their motivation is to be sustained throughout the process. The student should be able to identify, in a broad sense, what it is that they are interested in and why.

2.Carry out preliminary reading.

After deciding on a topic of interest students should undertake some general reading around the issue. Questions they must consider at this stage are:

- What has already been written about this topic?
- Was it easy to find sources of information?
- Is there a range of different sources available?
- Is there a range of views or perspectives on the topic?
- What interesting questions have started to emerge from this reading?

3.Consider the emerging questions.

The student should now begin posing open-ended questions about their general topic. These questions will usually be framed using the terms "how", "why" or "to what extent".

4.Evaluate the question.

Once possible research questions have been posed they should be evaluated. This evaluation should be based on whether the research question is clear, focused, and arguable.

Clear: Will the reader understand the nature of my research? Will it direct the research being undertaken?

Focused: Will the research question be specific enough to allow for exploration within the scope of the task (that is, the number of words and time available)?

Arguable: Does the research question allow for analysis, evaluation and the development of a reasoned argument?

5.Consider research outcomes.

Once a provisional research question has been decided upon students should start thinking about the direction their research might take. This could be in terms of:suggesting possible outcomes of the researchoutlining the kind of argument they might make and how the research might support thisconsidering options if the research available is not sufficient to support a sustained argument.

Derived From: Extended essay teacher support material (first assessment 2018)

HOW DO I CHOOSE A TOPIC?

One of the great things about doing an independent research piece is that you have the freedom to focus on almost any topic. It is not like other school essays or exams: you set the question yourself.

The subject area

Your research topic will fit into one of 6 specified subject areas:

- studies in language and literature
- individuals and societies
- mathematics
- the arts
- sciences
- language acquisition.

Make sure you understand which topic area your subject fits with, as this will help you decide on your sources and approach. For example, if you choose to examine the "causes of Brexit", you could look at it from political, economic, sociological, psychological or historical angles.

You can also do an extended essay in world studies which combines two subject areas to explore a topic of contemporary global significance.

Picking just one topic

You may have a list of possible topics. To narrow these down:

- Make sure your topic fits into one of the IB specified subject areas.
- Choose a topic that will keep you interested in for a long period of time.
- Try not to pick a topic that you have strong personal feelings about as you may not remain open-minded.
- Consider if there is a teacher who can supervise this topic.
- Make sure you have the resources you need to carry out your research.
- Consider choosing a topic which relates to your future career aspirations.

Once you have a possible topic in mind, you should start by getting an overview of the literature available.

You should take this literature as your starting point; you will evaluate it and build on it to reach your own conclusions. When you start your initial research, you should ask:

- What has already been written about this topic? A topic which has been researched extensively may not leave you with any gaps in current knowledge to fill, but if nobody has written about your topic it might not be worth investigating.
- Will it be easy to find sources of information? Some data and research is not readily accessible to the public and this could make it hard to gather information you need. Similarly, if you need access to a laboratory for experiments or people for a survey, you need to work out if this is going to be possible.
- Is there a range of different sources available? The most successful research projects draw on a variety of different sources types.
- Are there a range of views or perspectives on the topic? Many of the best research questions relate to a controversial issue which is the subject of debate. A topic like this will allow you to demonstrate critical thinking and reasoning abilities.
- Do you understand the key sources and concepts? If you find the sources difficult to understand, there's no shame in choosing a simpler topic. Some academic topics are only accessible to a very specialist audience.
- By addressing these questions, you can make sure you are making best use of your time and pursuing a question that is valid and practical.
- All research must be safe, ethical and appropriate so discuss your ideas with your supervisor before starting.
- **Remember to keep a record of your early ideas in your RRS as it shows how the student generated ideas and explored their area of interest from many different angles.**

Have your say:

What have been your first ideas for a project? Pick one idea and explain to your supervisor what makes it an appropriate topic for you to research or why you had to discard it.

Take the time to read other learners' postings, and comment on at least one idea that you find interesting. Use 'Like' to identify any posts that you find inspiring. You can sort the posts by 'Most liked' to view the most popular responses.

IDEA CLOUD

Without filtering or editing, write down all the hobbies you have, ways you like to spend your time, and topics you have strong opinions on (right now don't worry about relating it to your course)

If you need a bit of inspiration to select a topic, consider these questions:

- What problems do you want to solve?
- Make a list of the last five articles you have read in the news.
- If you were to write to the President, what is important to you to share? Have you been affected personally by a global issue?
- What was left out of a lesson that you want to know more about? Do you feel part of a story or perspective wasn't covered in a lesson?
- What do you want to learn that you have not covered in class?
- Have you heard a story about this topic from a family member and want to know more?
- What plans for further study or career do you have in mind?

TOP 3

Select your favourite or most interesting 3 ideas from your idea cloud here

IDEA 1

IDEA 2

IDEA 3

Pick the 2 most controversial of your topics and name two opposing positions (not necessarily those you agree with)

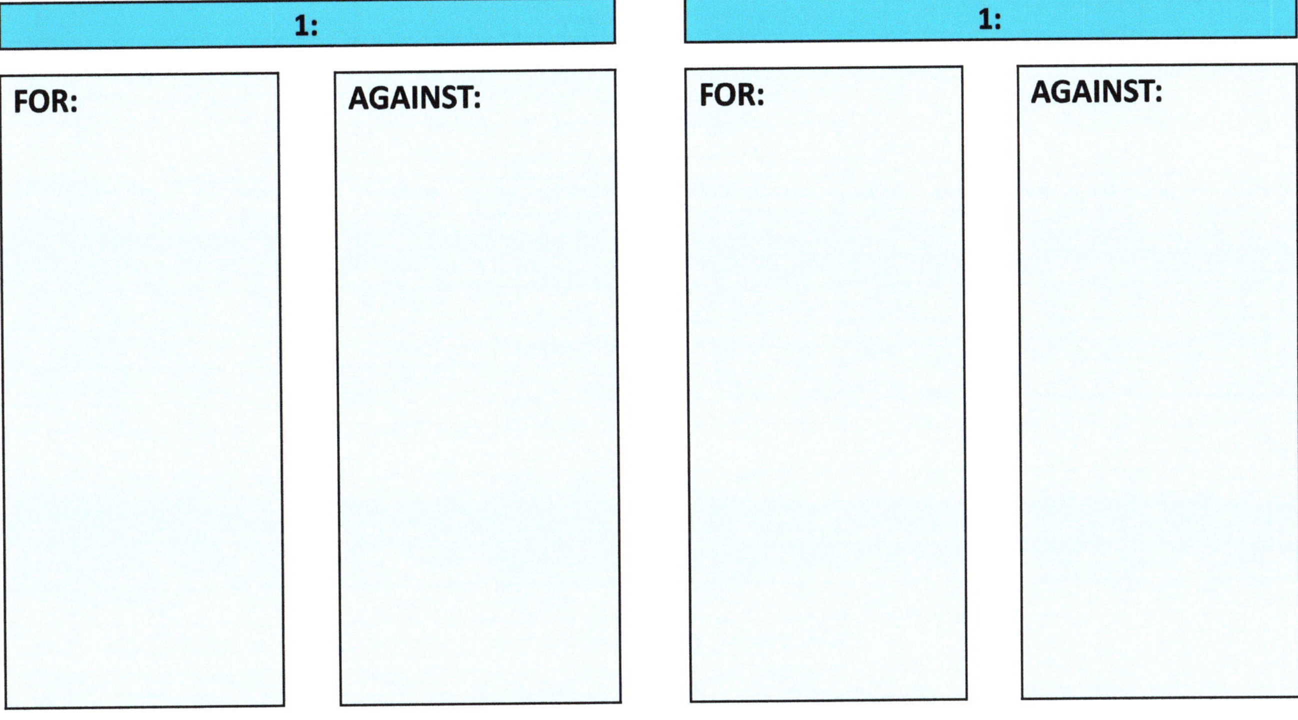

1:	
FOR:	AGAINST:

1:	
FOR:	AGAINST:

RESEARCH QUESTIONS

Below is a list of common question starters that may help you design your own RQ or convert a working title into a question format

Compare the poor research questions with the good questions in the table below. What improvements have been made?

Your research question (RQ) is the backbone of your essay. A good research question is:

- Phrased as a question
- Focused
- Allows for argument
- Feasible
- Able to be explored in enough depth in the time and word count

QUESTION STARTER	DESCRIPTION
To what extent...	Allows for an evaluation of the degree (extent) to which something is true or a contributing factor. To effectively answer this type of question, the main body of the essay should include considerations of other influencing factors. For example, a question relating to the extent to which the Spanish Constitution of 1931 caused the civil war of 1936 could potentially examine the role played by the military, external nations and other factors in order to more fully answer "the extent" aspect of the question.
Assess the role of...	Allows for an analysis of a specific factor or the contribution of something/ someone.
How accurate/reliable...	Allows for an exploration relating to the accuracy or usefulness.
How far could one argue...	Allows for the analysis to focus on the accuracy/ truthfulness of a specific argument or line of inquiry.
How successful...	Allows for an evaluation of the success of an approach, method, policy, style and so on an associated area (for example, success of a political policy on economic development of X region).
How crucial/significant...	Allows for an analysis of the significance of one or more factors on other associated areas.
Which factors played....	Allows for an investigation around key factors.
Has the introduction (or cancellation of)...resulted in...	Allows for a cause/effect-style investigation.
Does [X] process/approach provide...	Allows for a focused investigation on the result of a specific method followed or technique used.
What is the contribution/influence of...	Allows for a focused investigation on the impact (positive or negative) of a certain individual, group, material or concept on a broader area (eg, on a specific society).

QUESTION STARTER	DESCRIPTION
What evidence is there to support...	Allows for an investigation into the nature of evidence and the extent to which it can support a thesis or approach.
What is the impact of...	A straightforward causal investigation.
Is it possible to determine...	An investigation into hypothetical frameworks based on existing and available evidence.
Under what circumstances may...	Allows an investigation into the conditions required before X is deemed possible (for example, for a business to expand).
Is there a correlation between...	Allows for an investigation into the relationship between two or more factors.

Compare the poor research questions with the good questions in the table below. What improvements have been made?

POOR RQ	BETTER RQ
How racist are Disney's animated films from the 20th century?	To what extent does Disney successfully address its racist history from 'Song of the South' with 'The Princess and the Frog'?
What kinds of words gained new meaning during the 2020 Corona crisis?	To what extent does the language of Donald Trump during his Corona briefings in 2020 resemble the language of a political campaign?
How has Uber disrupted the taxi industry?	To what extent has the introduction of Uber in Amsterdam challenged employment laws in the taxi sector?
How do dimple patterns on golf balls affect ball flight?	To what extent are hexagon dimple patterns on golf balls effective for high-handicap golfers?
How are modern-day musicals inspired by operas?	To what extent does the musical language of Andrew Lloyd Weber take inspiration from classical opera of the eighteenth century?

YOUR RQ IDEA 1:

YOUR RQ IDEA 2:

FORMULATING A RESEARCH QUESTION

Developing a narrow, focused research question is an integral part of your extended essay process. A research question will provide a path to guide you through your research and writing

Step 1. Choose your subject area	*Which subject area is of most personal interest to you? Is there something you are especially curious about in one of your IB courses? Did one of your topics from an earlier grade spark an idea that can be researched?*
Step 2. Choose a topic that interests you	*Describe your work in one sentence.* I want to learn about ______________________. **Example:** I want to learn about public funding for the arts.
Step 3. Suggest a question	*Try to describe your research by developing a question that specifies something about your topic.* I am studying ______________________ because I want to find out (who, what, when, where, whether, why or how) ______________________. **Example**: I am studying public funding for the arts because I want to find out how accessible the arts are to those people who are on low incomes. **Direct question:** To what extent are the arts accessible to people who belong to the class of the working poor? Include a command term from your subject area to help form the research question. Will you be able to argue a specific position? What are some possible issues or arguments?
Step 4. Evaluate your question	*Answer the questions:* Is there a range of perspectives on this topic? Does the research question allow for analysis, evaluation and the development of a reasoned argument? I am studying ______________________ because I want to find out ______________________ in order to understand (how, why or whether) ______________________. **Example**: I am studying public funding for the arts because I want to find out how accessible the arts are to the working poor so I can determine whether tax dollars support cultural enrichment for all citizens regardless of their socio-economic status.
Step 5. Restate your question using a different command term	*Asking the question in a different way might help you view your topic in a different way. How does analyzing ...* *To what extent ...*
Step 6. Review with your supervisor	*Is your supervisor able to understand the nature of your research?* *Is it clear to your supervisor how and why your topic is relevant in your subject area?*
Step 7. Reflection	*If you can adequately respond to the "so what?" question, you may be on your way to a clear and focused research question using your initial topic idea.*

SUBJECT SPECIFIC DETAILS AND GUIDANCE

Your EE needs to be registered in one of the subjects available from the IB; ideally, one of the subjects you are taking and for WSEE any 2 subjects without any concurrence of tools, theories and models. Below are some key details for the most commonly chosen subject areas for our school. If you need information on other subjects, speak to Ms Kirsty or visit the EE web guide.

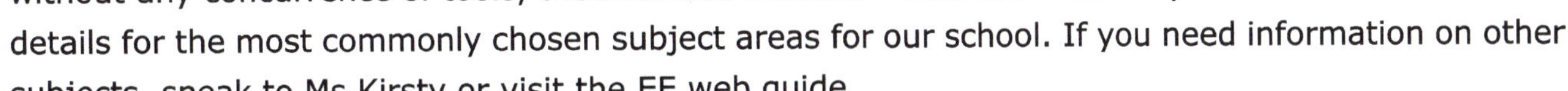

Language A

Category 1 - Studies of one or more literary works originally written in the language in which the essay is presented.

Category 2 - Studies of a literary work or works originally written in the language of the essay compared with one or more literary works originally written in another language. (The work originally written in another language may be studied in translation.)

Category 3 - Studies in language based on one or more texts originally produced in the language in which the essay is presented. Texts can be compared with a translated text originally written in another language.

Language B

Category 1 - A specific analysis of the language (its use and structure), normally related to its cultural context or a specific text.

Category 2 - An analysis of:

(a) the impact of a particular socio-cultural issue on the form or use of the language, based on an examination of language use

Or (b) a socio-cultural issue, as illustrated through specific cultural artefact(s) from a country/community where the language is spoken.

Category 3 - An analysis of a literary type, based on a specific work or works of literature exclusively from the target language.

History

The question should encourage an investigation that lends itself to analysis and critical commentary. Students should avoid straightforward "What" and "How" questions as they tend to lead to narrative treatment. Terms such as "How significant...?" or "How successful...?" are more likely to engage students in analysis.

"To what extent...?" requires an analytical answer, but if students choose this or a similar term, they need to ensure that their task does also require them to consider other factors to answer the question.

The topic must focus on the past and therefore be at least 10 years ago.

Business Management

The EE gives students an opportunity to develop research skills by:

- reviewing business theories, concepts and principles
- critically analysing their use and application in the business world and their resultant impact on business activity.

Students can choose a topic they have encountered during their Diploma Programme business management course.

However, they may also choose to investigate issues that fall outside its scope. For example:

- business practices in a specific regional or national context, or
- the practical applications of the work of a particular business management theorist.

Whatever area they choose, students must root their research firmly in accepted business management theories and use the core principles of business management as the basis for their research.

Biology

Biology is the science that deals with living organisms and life processes. A biology EE should incorporate biological theory and emphasize the essential nature of this subject. For example, an EE in an interdisciplinary area such as biochemistry will, if registered under the subject of biology, be judged solely on its biological content.

Some topics may be inadmissible because their means of investigation are unethical. For example, investigations that:

- are based on experiments likely to inflict pain on, or cause stress to, living organisms
- are likely to have a harmful effect on health, eg culturing micro-organisms at or near body temperature (37°C)
- involve access to, or publication of, confidential medical information.

In all cases where human subjects are used as the basis for an investigation, clear evidence of informed consent must be provided in accordance with the IB guidelines.

Some topics may be unsuitable because of safety issues. Adequate safety apparatus and qualified supervision is required for experiments involving dangerous substances such as:

- toxic or dangerous chemicals
- carcinogenic substances
- radioactive materials.

Other topics may be unsuitable because the outcome is already well known and documented in standard textbooks.

Chemistry

Chemistry is the science that deals with the composition, characterization and transformation of substances. A chemistry EE should incorporate chemical principles and theory, and emphasize the study of matter and of the changes it undergoes. For example, an EE in an option area of the IB syllabus such as biochemistry will, if registered as a chemistry EE, be judged on its content within the scope of the biochemistry option of the syllabus.

Broad or complex literature-based topics do not allow the student to discuss conflicting ideas and theories, nor to produce an in-depth personal analysis within the word limit. Students should therefore avoid these topics (eg investigations into health problems caused by water pollution, chemotherapy for cancer treatment or the use of spectroscopy in chemical analysis).

Some topics may be unsuitable for investigation because of safety issues. Experiments involving toxic or dangerous chemicals, carcinogenic substances or radioactive materials should be avoided unless adequate safety apparatus and qualified supervision are available and evaluation of the level of risk has been positively determined. Teachers are responsible for following national or local guidelines, which may differ from country to country.

Other topics may be unsuitable because the outcome is already well known and documented in standard textbooks.

Visual Arts

The visual arts are here broadly defined also to include architecture, design and contemporary forms of visual culture.

The research may be generated or inspired by the student's direct experiences of creating visual artworks, or by their interest in the work of a particular artist, style or period. This might be related to the student's own cultural context or another cultural context.

Personal contact with artists, curators and other active participants in the visual arts is encouraged, as is the use of local and primary sources.

Students must avoid topics that are overly broad or descriptive in nature, such as one that covers many aspects of art history or particularly long periods of time or biographies of artists. The topic must relate directly to the visual arts.

Film

Students should undertake the study of at least two films/major television works in consideration of their chosen topic. The EE requires students to develop and demonstrate a critical understanding of how and why film texts:

- tell stories
- create emotional responses
- give information.

In the spirit of intercultural understanding, students are encouraged to explore film in an international context.

The topic must clearly focus on film or television, rather than a literary, sociological, political or historical issue. For example, a study of film adaptations of Shakespeare's plays or of classic novels must not become a literature essay about the plays or the novels. It must be a discussion about the films from a filmic point of view.

If addressing a topic already addressed in academic studies, students must examine existing views and argue against them to some degree. Earlier studies must be used as a basis for discussion and not be merely

World Studies

An EE in world studies gives students the opportunity to undertake an interdisciplinary study of an issue of contemporary global significance. "Interdisciplinary" in this context refers to research that draws on the methods, concepts and theories of two Diploma Programme subjects. It is strongly recommended that students are undertaking a course of study in at least one of the subjects chosen for their essay. "Contemporary" in this context refers to events that took place during the student's lifetime.

Students are required to:

- identify an issue of global importance
- identify a local manifestation of the issue of global importance
- develop a clear rationale for taking an interdisciplinary approach and use the conceptual framework and vocabulary of two Diploma Programme subjects.

This provides an opportunity for students to conduct independent interdisciplinary research (not necessarily primary research) that draws on Diploma Programme subjects and integrates them to produce a coherent and insightful analysis of the global issue they choose to investigate. It should be noted that law and education are not Diploma Programme subjects.

World studies EEs are registered in one of six areas of study: these are not the same as the Diploma Programme subjects. They are:

- **Conflict, peace and security Culture, language and identity**
- **Environmental and/or economic sustainability Equality and inequality**
- **Health and development Science, technology and society.**

The interdisciplinary essay is designed to provide students with the opportunity to:

- engage in, and pursue, a systematic process of research appropriate to the topic—a process that is Informed by knowledge, concepts, theories, perspectives and methods from two chosen subjects develop research and communication skills—including the ability to communicate with readers who have a background in more than one subject or discipline
- develop the skills of creative and critical thinking—particularly those skills involved in integrating concepts, theories, perspectives, findings or examples from different subjects to develop new insights or understandings
- experience the excitement of intellectual discovery—including insights into how different subjects complement or challenge one another when used to address the same topic or issue.

Furthermore, in line with the IB's mission, the world studies EE seeks to advance students' emerging global consciousness. This comprises:

- a sensitivity to local phenomena as manifestations of broader developments on the planet the capacity to think in flexible and informed ways in understanding issues of global significance a developing perception of the student's own identity (self) as a global actor and member of humanity, capable of making a positive contribution to the world.

PROPOSAL FORM

Name: ____________________

Proposed topic: ____________________

____

____

Proposed RQ: ____________________

____

____

Subject this would be registered under: ____________________

Subjects you are studying at HL: ____________________

____

Subjects you are studying at SL: ____________________

____

What are your future study or career plans: ____________________

____

____

____

Why you think this topic and question are worthy of study: ____________________

____

____

____

What you already know about the topic and RQ:

____

____

____

What you think or hope to find out about the topic and RQ:

____

____

____

RESEARCH

What is research?

Go back to your notes on the ATL skills and the assessment criteria.

In what ways is research like booking a holiday or planning an event?

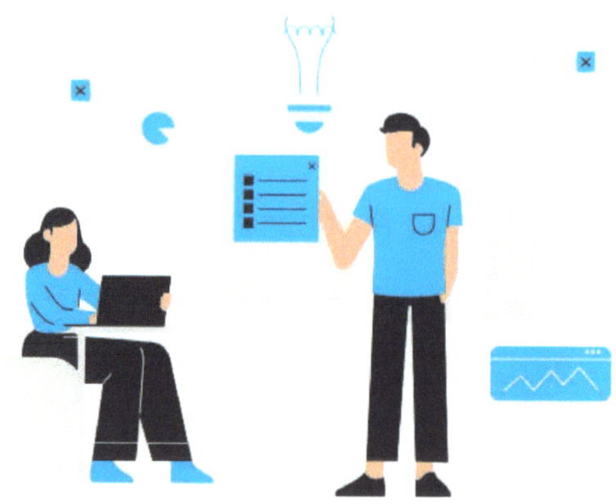

PRIMARY SOURCES	SECONDARY SOURCES

Note that a book is simply a format. You can find primary *and* secondary sources published in book form.

When planning your research, consider:

- What do you already know?
- What do you need to know to answer your question?
- Where can you locate these answers or how can you find them out?

METHODOLOGY

Your methodology is how you plan to answer your question. There are a number of approaches (methods) you can take and you may use more than one.

Experiment

You may wish to investigate by testing your hypothesis or theory for yourself. This is particularly effective for science-based EEs. Make sure you consider the ethical standards of any experiments, which you can find in the IB documentation.

Questionnaire or Survey

To collect short pieces of information from a large group of people, a questionnaire or survey is helpful. Make sure the questions you ask are clear and measurable. You can hand out paper copies or use an online tool as Google Forms or Survey Monkey.

Interview

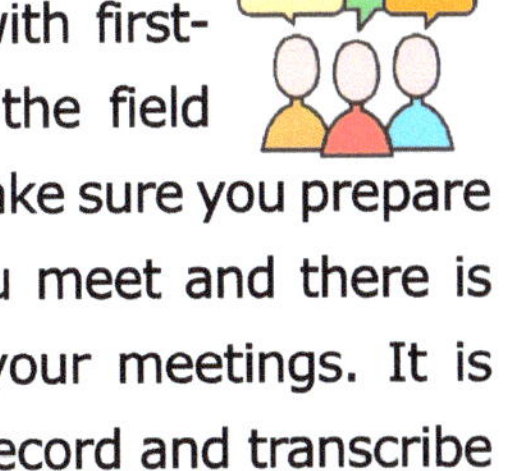

You may wish to speak to (an) expert(s) or those with first-hand experience in the field you are exploring. Make sure you prepare questions before you meet and there is consistency across your meetings. It is also a good idea to record and transcribe your meetings to make it easier to use quotations from these experts.

Articles

It may be that someone has already conducted similar research to you. You should read what has already been written about your subject and can use this as a basis to explain why you have or haven't taken a particular approach. Official articles are 'peer-reviewed' and published on reputable databases but be sure to consider any other biases that may be present.

Documents and Records

You may need to collect first-hand accounts or policies on your chosen topic, such as diary entries, news articles or reports. This may involve accessing paper or digital archives and are useful for seeing the impact an event has on individuals or the intention of particular companies.

Case Studies

You may wish to focus on a particular individual, company or situation in close detail with a number of factors to consider. These may be of particular use in business or economical essays that focus on the different elements that have led to a particular outcome. This may be someone that you have a connection to for ease of access to information or a large company with details that are easily accessible in the public domain.

REMEMBER

It is important to get **informed consent** from anyone you are collecting data from so that they know what to expect and what you plan to use the information for.

You should also make sure you keep details anonymous and confidential (unless you discover something that you think is important to be shared, such as a safe-guarding issue).

CONDUCTING RESEARCH

Applying a critical analysis framework to research

This framework provides prompts for key questions to ask about the quality and rigour of the work under consideration. The process is not rigid and can be adapted to suit a wide range of types of research and scholarly work.

Identify the intention

Reading the abstract is the fastest way to determine this. Try dividing your reading into three categories: that which requires more detailed reading and analysis; that which can easily be discarded as not relevant; and that which requires more consideration before it can be included or discarded.

Identify the main ideas

Ideally, the research questions will be clearly set out in one of the first few sections of the paper. If not, then the researcher will pose the questions at various intervals during the paper. There is also the conclusion section where the main ideas will once again be articulated.

Identify the underlying theoretical and methodological approaches

If there is a methodology section, it's normally here that you find the theoretical approach taken by the researcher. This should let you know the epistemological and ontological basis of the research, and it will allow you to understand how it fits with your own approach.

What evidence is presented to support the arguments?

How does the author support their main argument(s)? What evidence do they provide (qualitative or quantitative)? Is the evidence strong or weak? In this step the quality of the evidence can also be assessed.

The 'so what?' test

All the time you are reading research you will need to be going back to the notion of why you need the research you are reading and how it will add to your overall understanding. If it does neither then you will need to reject the research; if it does one or the other, it's worth looking again and seeing whether the other question could be applied.

What questions does the article prompt?

Good research will prompt the reader to consider further questions. The best research will either pose further related questions or indicate where there is more research to do or different avenues to investigate.

from *Doing Your Education Research Project*

Creating an annotated bibliography

An annotated bibliography provides a concise summary of each source and some assessment of its value and relevance. It is excellent preparation for carrying out independent research.

Annotated bibliography—its function

The process is not just a matter of listing possible sources. It also requires you to think critically. Consider your sources in terms of:

- what has already been written about their chosen topic and
- how your own research will fit into this.

As you examine each source, you will need to identify the issues and different perspectives of others. This will help you to develop a reasoned argument.

A good annotated bibliography will:

- allow you to keep track of your reading
- encourage you to think critically about the sources you are using in relation to your research area
- allow you, quite early on in the process, to become aware of possible concerns about using certain sources
- help you determine whether a source is of use to you in your research
- help you to justify your use of particular sources, both to your supervisor and to the IB examiner who will be reading your essay
- help you with the planning of your research, and **ultimately save your time**
- enable you to develop critical-thinking skills in selecting and evaluating source material.

TIP: The annotated bibliography is a planning tool to help you manage your research and time. It must not be included in the EE as an appendix.

Popular journal databases:

- JSTOR
- EBSCO
- Taylor and Francis
- SpringerLink
- ERIC
- DOAJ
- Semantic Scholar

ANNOTATED BIBLIOGRAPHY TEMPLATE

PEER PRESENTATIONS

Title: Author: Date of publication: Location of publication: Publisher: If online, URL and date(s) accessed:
Summary of key findings:
Key Quotations (with page no.)
Biases or other things to consider:

PEER PRESENTATIONS

Although your supervisor is your first port of call for the work on your EE, it is helpful to seek feedback from other sources.

Therefore, you will create a present a run-down of your work so far to the rest of the class. This will be followed by questions from the class on your work and a chance to discuss key parts of your process.

What does a good presentation look like?

Your chosen area and why you selected it

I chose to write my EE on the artist Banksy because...

Your research question or area of focus and why you think it is worth investigating

I am exploring the allegorical aspect of his work because...

What kinds of research you have conducted and what this has taught you

I have used YouTube videos, news reports and his autobiography because. . .

How the research will help you answer the question or how it has affected your opinion of the topic or question

This has shown me that . . .Initially I thought . . . But now I believe . . .

What you still need to do

I am still missing . . .Therefore . . .

What you have learnt during the process (study skills, time management, etc)

The most difficult thing for me has been . . . Now I need to . . .because . . .

PLANNING THE EXTENDED ESSAY

EXAMPLE OUTLINE

OUTLINE	NOTES
I. Thesis: Japanese theater rose from a popular to elite and then returned to a popular art form.	The thesis is stated in the first section, which is the introduction. NOTE: In an IB Extended Essay, the introduction must include the research question.
II. Early theatrical forms A. Bugaku B. Sarugaku C. Primitive Noh D. Authors and Audience **III. Noh theater** A. Authors B. Props 1. Masks a. women b. demons c. old men 2. Structure of Stage C. Themes 1. Buddhist influence 2. The supernatural D. Kyogen interludes E. Audience **IV. Kabuki** A. Authors B. Props 1. make-up 2. special effects C. Themes 1. Love stories 2. Revenge D. Audience **V. Bunraku (puppet) theater** A. Authors B. Props C. Themes 1. Love stories 2. Historical romances D. Audience	The body follows the introduction, and breaks down the points the author wishes to make. Note that some sections have subdivisions, others do not, depending on the demands of the paper. In this outline, II, III, & IV all have similar structure, but this will not necessarily be true for all papers. Some may only have three major sections, others more than the five given here.
VI. Conclusion	Your conclusion should restate your thesis, and never introduce new material. NOTE: In an IB Extended Essay, the conclusion must provide an answer to the research question first stated in the introduction.

WRITING THE EXTENDED ESSAY

THE INTRODUCTION

- Ideally should not be more than 10% of your essay
- Outlines what you have chosen (explicitly state your question and that it matches your cover page)
- Explains why you have chosen this question
- Explains the approach you have chosen and why
- Identifies your position

Introduction & bibliography
Criterion B and C

- Appropriate use of subject knowledge & terms
- Clearly developed argument
- Based on the evidence
- Critical reflection of research

  Main body & conclusion

Use the PEA structure:

- Point - What is your opinion/idea? What are you trying to say?
- Evidence – Give a quotation or example to support you
- Analysis – how and why does this support you? How does it help to prove your overall argument?

THE CONCLUSION

- Ideally should not be more than 10% of your essay
- Restates your purpose and hypothesis
- Summarises findings or points, without repeating
- Explains the bigger picture or "so what?"
- Considers the limitations and prospect for further research

Criterion A

- Research question must be clear, focused but not too narrow & allow for an argument
- Range, suitability & reliability of sources
- Approach

MAIN BODY

- You have collected a range of relevant primary and secondary sources
- You have explained the relevance and importance of your research and sources
- Evidence supports your argument rather than your points summarising the evidence
- Explains why this evidence supports you and why it is important
- You relate what you are saying back to your research question
- You have an argument that links your points together rather than just a list of points
- You use sections and subheadings to show the progression of your argument

A project conclusion has two main functions: it should refer back to what you have written, reminding the reader of your argument, and giving some sort of evaluation and/or interpretation; and it should point forward to what you think might happen in the future, with suggestions or recommendations, or predictions or warnings.

from *Academic Essay Writing for Postgraduates*

Ace Criterion C

Critically analysing sources

Critical thinking is an essential research skill, especially for completing the IB Diploma, but what is it and how can you get better at it?

When examiners read your extended essay and Reflections on Planning and Progress Form, they will look closely at the process you have taken to reach your final conclusions.

They will examine:

- how and why you have chosen to use certain sources
- if your work is sufficiently informed and supported by evidence
- how you have justified your arguments.

All of these demonstrate key critical thinking skills which are useful in the IB, at university and beyond.

Of the assessment criteria, critical thinking is weighted the most heavily. You could earn up to 12 marks: this is 35% of the available total.

You can demonstrate your critical thinking by:

- carefully selecting and analysing the sources and data used to inform your research
- developing your own clear and well-reasoned argument in direct response to the research question.

You will focus on the first area in this step and the second in the following step.

What is critical writing?

Critical writing is different as it actively develops your argument. When you write critically you will evaluate the work of others and their interpretations, and analyse key concepts, issues or ideas. You assess different views, make reasoned judgements based on evidence and draw your own conclusions. In short, critical writing is where you can best showcase your originality and ability to craft an informed argument.

Here is an example from an essay examining the Arab Spring movement in 2011:

Descriptive writing	Critical writing
Nation-wide protests on the 25th January 2011 marked a key turning point in the Egyptian revolution, which ultimately led to the resignation of President Hosni Mubarak on the 11th February.	A popular uprising in Tunisia in December 2010 sparked a similar movement in Egypt, protesting against rampant corruption, poor governance and a lack of democratic process. These events are significant in that they represented a major catalyst for the broader Arab Spring throughout early 2011.

The description merely states events as they occurred, whereas the analysis looks for links between events and explains their wider significance.

How to select and analyse sources

It involves keeping an open mind about the information you encounter, whilst also identifying misleading, inaccurate or biased sources.

This will become easier over time as you gain background knowledge about your subject and an understanding of what makes a good information source.

Just because there is bias or inaccuracy in a source does not mean you cannot use it in your research. However, it is important that you point out any issues with the source and explain why you have still included it. For example, primary sources like witness accounts will carry an inherent level of bias. You must show your awareness of this, and address it in your essay.

Equally, you should analyse any academic research you include in your essay. Sometimes we accept academic sources without questioning them simply because they are 'academic'. However, your examiner will be looking at how you have demonstrated critical thinking when using these sources. So, don't be afraid to evaluate academic research and point to its limitations.

Ultimately, you are responsible for reaching conclusions about each individual information source you use.

You might find it hard to think critically in this context. But, you are probably already using these skills in your daily life. For instance, you may be skeptical about promises made by politicians. You probably already notice when friends share unsubstantiated claims on the internet. And it's likely that you know that a meme is not a reliable source of information. These are critical thinking skills: use and develop them through your research.

To help you get started, ask yourself these questions when analysing sources:

- What is the context of this source? You should consider these issues: when was it written, who wrote it, where was it published and why were they writing it?
- Is there any evidence to support its claims?
- Are the conclusions drawn from this source verified by a wide range of other literature?

As you go through this process, you will see that not all sources are useful or reliable. Don't be afraid to discard those that you don't need. Some sources should be avoided altogether. Wikipedia is a good example since there is no guarantee that the information is accurate. However, it can be a good starting point. See the Downloads section for guidance on conducting a literature review.

As you collect and discard your sources, record your activity in your Researcher's Reflection Space (RRS) and ultimately on the Reflections on Planning and Progress Form. It will help you keep track of your critical thinking and provide evidence to the examiner.

What is a good argument?

What makes a good argument? How can you ensure that the arguments you are making are valid and persuasive?

There are five main guidelines worth following to help you to develop an effective argument.

1. Acknowledge alternative perspectives

It's easy to see things in black-and-white and fall heavily on one side or the other, but it is not helpful to view issues in this way. There is rarely a "right" or "wrong" answer to something. Even scientists can interpret the same data in different ways or use differing methods. Often, there are valid viewpoints on either side of a debate or multiple possible interpretations of an event or idea. In fact, it is probably this ambiguity or controversy which makes your topic worth exploring.

Examiners will assess if you have considered alternative interpretations and ideas. You are not undermining your own argument if you acknowledge counter-arguments. In fact, you can strengthen your own point if you explain why counter-arguments are weak or unjustified.

2. Support arguments with reliable evidence

In most cases, you will need to include evidence, examples or data to support the claims you make. In some cases, a reference to where you found the data will suffice. Remember, if any of your arguments rely on biased, non-credible or inaccurate sources, then those arguments will not be persuasive.

3. Make arguments relevant: answer the question

It may sound obvious, but it's important to ensure that every point you make helps you answer the main research question. Your essay will be made up of a series of points which all play a meaningful role in the development of your overall argument: you should not make any points which are irrelevant to your final conclusion.

4. Be consistent: do not contradict yourself

Examiners look for a clear line of argument that is sustained throughout. You cannot change your mind halfway through the essay as it will confuse your reader and make your final argument less convincing. Moreover, you should make it clear where you are using your **own** argument in the language you use.

5. Ensure arguments are based on good logic: avoid logical fallacies

Arguments are based on reasons (or premises) which are either implied or explicit. If the premise is flawed or does not lead logically to the conclusion, then your argument will not be persuasive. Flawed arguments are sometimes called **logical fallacies**. You might encounter these types of arguments in the media, or conversation: some are easier to notice than others.

Having an awareness of common fallacies can help you identify flaws in your own reasoning as well in the arguments of those around you. You can see examples of fallacies and get advice on how you can avoid making the same mistakes by downloading 'Common fallacies' in the Downloads section.

The importance of an open mind

Keeping an open mind means questioning other people's views and your own. By questioning ideas, you can make your writing more objective and develop more persuasive arguments based on reason and evidence. You will be practising this skill while studying the Theory of Knowledge part of your IB Diploma, so you can apply it as you write your essay.

Have your say:

- Can you give some examples of flawed arguments you have encountered?
- Can you think of any arguments you found convincing even though it turned out they were inaccurate?

Share your thoughts with your Supervisor.

Deciding on which arguments to include

Once you have collected all your ideas into one place, assess your arguments to decide which ones to include:

1. Pick out the most relevant points: make sure they all play a meaningful role in answering the main question. If a point isn't essential to your argument or isn't very persuasive, leave it out.
2. Make sure the points you want to include are all backed up with sufficient evidence. If you do not have any evidence to back up your points, do not include them.
3. Think about what your reader needs to know. Do not include too much background material. Remember to ask yourself: does this answer the question?

Once you have identified the main points you want to include, consider the order you want to present them in. You may want to present information thematically, chronologically or starting general and getting more specific. It all depends on your own individual argument and how you feel it can be presented most logically.

Structuring individual body paragraphs

The PEE method of structuring individual paragraphs can help ensure each point is made persuasively:

- **Point**: a statement, claim or assertion you want to make.
- **Evidence**: information, or an example which supports the point.
- **Explanation**: the reason, logic or justification for the point.

If appropriate, you can use headings to help separate your writing into distinct sections. This helps the reader follow the flow of your essay

Check your understanding

What type of logical fallacy is this?

"Antony Smith's recent article on the environment and conservation is a load of rubbish. He chooses his own private car over public transport and he's not even a vegetarian: his ideas are nonsense."

- ☐ *Ad hominem*
- ☐ Slippery slope
- ☐ Circular argument
- ☐ Appeal to ignorance
- ☐ False dichotomy

Submit answer: ***Ad hominem***

Ad hominem, literally meaning "to the person", is where someone argues against a point by attacking the person who said it rather than the argument itself. Just because Antony Smith drives a car and eats meat, does not mean his article on conservation is not academically sound or viable. The article must be judged on its own merits.

What type of logical fallacy is this?

"According to recent data provided by the government of Uzbekistan, 80% of the population believe that climate change is not a result of human activity. Therefore climate change must have been caused by something else."

- ☐ Slippery slope
- ☐ Appeal to the majority
- ☐ Hasty generalisation
- ☐ Causal fallacy
- ☐ Appeal to emotion

Ans: An "appeal to the majority" (*ad populum*) fallacy is where someone claims that something is true on the basis that many people believe it to be so. However, just because many people believe something, this does not mean it is necessarily true or correct. The fact that the majority of Uzbekistan's population believe that climate change is not caused by human activity, does not prove that human activity does not cause climate change.

What type of logical fallacy is this?

"If plastic bags are banned, what next? Before you know it plastic bottles will be illegal and we'll all be dehydrated. Takeaway boxes will be banned so we'll all be hungry."

- ☐ Appeal to authority
- ☐ Hasty generalisation
- ☐ False cause
- ☐ Slippery slope
- ☐ Circular argument

Ans: The "slippery slope" fallacy is where someone argues against something by trying to demonstrate that it will end in dire consequences. These dire consequences, however, do not follow on logically from the premise. In this case, the author assumes that a simple ban on plastic bags will somehow lead to everyone being dehydrated and hungry. This is an exaggerated and illogical conclusion.

What type of logical fallacy is this?

"After the Fukushima radiation leak, the population of starfish on the East coast of the United States experienced a dramatic decline. Therefore the Fukushima radiation leak was responsible for the demise of the starfish."

- ☐ Hasty generalisation
- ☐ Appeal to emotion
- ☐ False cause
- ☐ Slippery slope
- ☐ Appeal to ignorance

Ans: The false cause (*post hoc ergo propter hoc*, literally meaning "after this, therefore because of this") fallacy identifies a correlation between two events and assumes that one caused the other. In this case, the author is assuming that the Fukushima disaster caused the death of starfish on the Eastern coast of America. However, there is no conclusive proof to link these two events together: just because one event occurred before another does not mean the first caused the second.

How can you make sure that your writing style will enable you to succeed in your extended essay?

One way of doing this is to ensure that you are writing critically rather than descriptively.

Last week, you explored the importance of setting up a good research question. Your research question can make all the difference in how you write your essay. A good question allows you to write an essay which uses critical thinking skills to reach original conclusions, but a poor question might lead you to merely describe what has already been said about your topic.

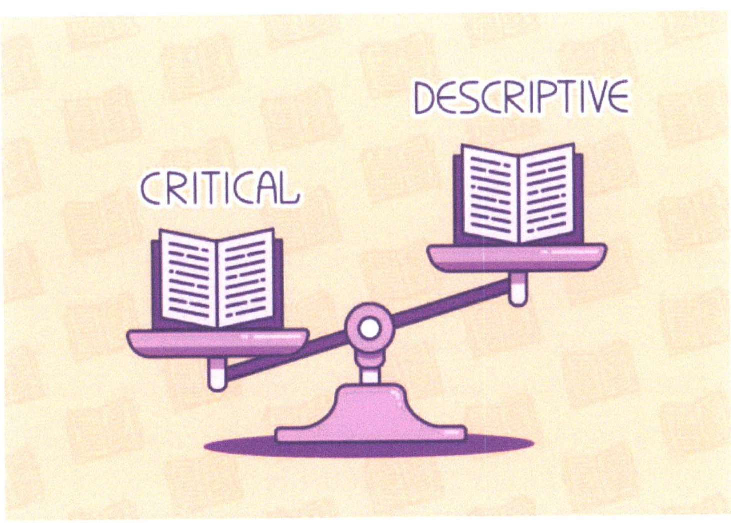

Question 1

Which is an example of critical writing?

- **Extract A:**

"The percentage of live coral cover on reefs in Mo'orea, French Polynesia, recovers quickly from disturbance events such as cyclones or coral bleaching."

- **Extract B:**

"The rapid recovery of live coral cover in Mo'orea suggests that the reefs are healthy in spite of climate change. However, using coral cover as the only indicator of reef health is not sufficient, because it does not look at how the species composition of the coral population may be changing."

Ans: Extract B demonstrates critical analysis:

"The rapid recovery of live coral cover in Mo'orea suggests that the reefs are healthy in spite of climate change. However, using coral cover as the only indicator of reef health is not sufficient, because it does not look at how the species composition of the coral population may be changing."

Critical writing looks at the limitations of research data and explores multiple possible causes for an event or occurrence.

Here, the writer acknowledges when there is not enough evidence to make a claim. Using tentative verbs such as 'suggests', 'may' and 'could explain', helps you assert the likelihood of your argument, whilst acknowledging that it cannot be proven conclusively.

Question 2

Which is an example of critical writing?

- **Extract A**

"DNA was isolated from a patient tumour sample, and was sequenced using the Sanger sequencing technique. This revealed a mutation in the target gene. An online database of somatic mutations was consulted and showed that this mutation is present in around 60% of the general population."

- **Extract B:**

"Although Sanger sequencing revealed a mutation in the target gene, this mutation is present in around 60% of the general population with no apparent health implications. This suggests that there is no clinical significance for this mutation, and so does not provide any further insight into the cause of disease. Further investigation of other genetic mutations would therefore be warranted."

Ans: Extract B demonstrates critical analysis:

"Although Sanger sequencing revealed a mutation in the target gene, this mutation is present in around 60% of the general population with no apparent health implications. This suggests that there is no clinical significance for this mutation, and so does not provide any further insight into the cause of disease. Further investigation of other genetic mutations would therefore be warranted."

Rather than simply describing how the DNA sequencing was carried out and what the results were, the critical example also explains the significance of the results.

The writer shows that the sequencing has not helped provide any further insight into the cause of the disease because most of the population has the mutation. They therefore explain the limitations of the study and express the need for further investigation.

Which is an example of critical writing?

- **Extract A:**

"The characterisation of the handsome lapiths and the grotesque centaurs suggests a fight between good and evil. It seems likely that this depiction was designed to reflect the recent victory of the Greeks over the "barbaric" Persians. Therefore, the sculpture on the Parthenon could be seen as a kind of political propaganda."

- **Extract B:**

"The sculpture on south side of the Parthenon depicts Centaurs fighting Lapiths. This was based on a popular mythological story. In the sculpture the centaur is seen with big, bulging eyes, a large nose and no neck. The Lapiths appear handsome and muscular"

Ans: *Extract A demonstrates critical analysis:*

"The characterisation of the handsome lapiths and the grotesque centaurs suggests a fight between good and evil. It seems likely that this depiction was designed to reflect the recent victory of the Greeks over the "barbaric" Persians. Therefore, the sculpture on the Parthenon could be seen as a kind of political propaganda."

Rather than simply describing the appearance of the sculpture, critical writing involves interpreting the sculpture and explaining its wider significance.

Completing the IB extended essay is a great opportunity to practice academic writing – an essential skill for university.

Academic writing is clear, concise, focussed, structured and informed by evidence. It is designed to aid the reader's understanding. It has a formal tone, but is not complex and does not require long sentences and complicated vocabulary.

There are many features of academic writing. It:

- is formal in tone
- uses simple vocabulary
- uses short sentences
- is concise and to-the-point
- includes linking phrases to signpost the reader (eg 'however' and 'therefore').

In your writing, try to avoid:

- hyperbolic language (exaggerations and sensationalist claims)
- emotive language
- 'flowery' or convoluted language
- repetition
- vague and lengthy sentences.

To help you develop your academic writing you might like to follow these top tips:

- **Reading widely** will build your vocabulary and understanding of academic style. You can then apply this to your own writing.
- If you are having difficulty expressing something in writing, try **saying it out loud** as if you were explaining it to someone else. This may help you explain an idea clearly and in a grammatically correct way.
- Make sure you set aside a good amount of time for **editing** your work. When you edit, look for words or even sentences that don't add anything or repeat ideas; you want to make every word count.
- Always **proofread** your work and ideally get someone else to check for spelling mistakes and to identify areas where your argument is not clear.

Further your understanding:

This exercise is designed to help you reflect on the different features of academic writing.

An example of a body paragraph from an extended essay:

Find out more about the different aspects of academic language the extract demonstrates

Question: To what extent did the First World War change perceptions about the roles of women in England during the period 1914-1930?

Although it might be argued that women's employment status greatly improved as a result of the First World War, it is evident that the war did little to close the gender gap. Women assumed a number of vital roles in the workforce, with over a million taking up employment between 1914 and 1918. There were a number of new opportunities women pursued including careers in the civil service, transport, and metal or chemical manufacturing. **Of these, the civil service provided women with an unparalleled opportunity to gain employment.** Contemporary research into the statistics for the period suggests that the number of women employed in roles such as typists within the civil service, increased by 1,751% and the number employed in other civil services branches such as the post office increased by 100% (Barton, 1919, p.534). **However, although access to opportunities may have increased, gender inequality remained an issue in respect of parity in pay.** Research (Crew, 1989) has indicated that women working in munitions factories earned significantly less than men. **Moreover, while legal change such as the Sex Disqualification Act of 1919 intended to make it illegal to exclude women from employment on the basis of the gender, in practice women's roles in their new employment were rarely secure.** The Restoration of Pre-War Practices Act of 1919 which encouraged factories to return to pre-war practices, meant that many women were forced out their jobs which were given to soldiers returning from duty. Scholars have shown that 'women workers acquiesced in this attempt to restore the prewar status quo' (Woollacott, 1994, p.109) which suggests that little had changed as a result of the war. While the First World War may have changed perceptions about the role of women, the impact of these changes was often short-lived and underlying inequality still existed.

On this page you can see an example of a body paragraph from an extended essay. **On this page you can see an example of a body paragraph from an extended essay.**

The significance of using academic language

Completing the IB extended essay is a great opportunity to practice academic writing – an essential skill for university.

Academic writing is clear, concise, focused, structured and informed by evidence. It is designed to aid the reader's understanding. It has a formal tone, but is not complex and does not require long sentences and complicated vocabulary.

There are many features of academic writing. It:

- is formal in tone
- uses simple vocabulary
- uses short sentences
- is concise and to-the-point
- includes linking phrases to signpost the reader (eg 'however' and 'therefore').

In your writing, try to avoid:

- hyperbolic language (exaggerations and sensationalist claims)
- emotive language
- 'flowery' or convoluted language
- repetition
- vague and lengthy sentences.

To help you develop your academic writing you might like to follow these top tips.

- **Reading widely** will build your vocabulary and understanding of academic style. You can then apply this to your own writing.
- If you are having difficulty expressing something in writing, try **saying it out loud** as if you were explaining it to someone else. This may help you explain an idea clearly and in a grammatically correct way.
- Make sure you set aside a good amount of time for **editing** your work. When you edit, look for words or even sentences that don't add anything or repeat ideas; you want to make every word count.
- Always **proofread** your work and ideally get someone else to check for spelling mistakes and to identify areas where your argument is not clear.

By this point, you probably have an idea about what topic you want to investigate for your extended essay.

REFERENCING

Any information or ideas that are not your own must be referenced, both at the point of use (known as "in-text citations") and in a list of at the end of your essay (known as a "reference list" or "works cited" page)..

There are a number of different reference styles you can choose from. It doesn't matter which one you use but you MUST use it consistently. Some styles are used more commonly in particular subjects so check with your supervisor or Ms Kirsty if you aren't sure which one is best.

Documentation checklist	
When you have used an author's exact words, have you put "quotation marks" around the quotation **and** named (cited) the original writer?	☐
(If you indent your quotation(s), quotation marks are not needed, but the, author must still be cited; have you cited your indented quotations?)	☐
When you put someone else's thoughts and ideas in your own words, have you still named I (cited) the original author(s)?	☐
When you use someone else's words or work, is it clear where such use starts—and where it finishes?	☐
I Have you included full references for all borrowed images, tables, graphs, maps, and so on?	☐
Print material: Have you included the page number(s) of print material you have used (especially important with exact quotations)?	☐
Internet material: Have you included both the date on which the, material was posted **and** the date of your last visit to the web page or site?	☐
Internet material: Have you included the URL or the DOI?	☐
For each citation in the text, is there a full reference in your list of references (works citied/ bibliography) at the end? Is the citation a direct link to the first word(s) of the reference?	☐
For each reference in the list of references, (works cited/bibliography) at the end, is there a citation in the text?	☐
Do(es) the first word(s) of the reference link directly to the citation as used?	☐
Is your list of references (works cited/bibliography) in alphabetical order, with the last name of the author first?	☐

REFERENCING

In-Text Citations

The three main types of in-text citation are as follows.

1. Author In-text citation is done by an introductory and/or parenthetical citation providing:
   - the last name of the author, and
   - page number(s) from which the quotation or paraphrase is taken, if applicable.
2. Author–date In-text citation is done by an introductory and/or parenthetical citation providing:
   - the last name of the author, and
   - the year of publication from which the quotation or paraphrase is taken, and the page number, if applicable.
3. Numbered footnote In-text citation is done by:
   - superscript note numbers that come after the referenced passage, and after the final punctuation mark, if used, and
   - corresponding footnotes placed at the bottom of their page of reference containing all reference details from which the quotation or paraphrase is taken; when using a source for a second or subsequent time, a shorter footnote reference is sufficient.

from *Effective Citing and Referencing*, p. 5

Reference List
At the end of the EE should be a list of all the sources you have referred to in your essay. Depending on which reference format you are using, these may have a different heading. However, as a minimum, this should include:
- Author's name
- Year published
- Title
- Edition (if applicable)
- Place of publication
- Publisher
- If online, URL and most recent date accessed

At Codrington, we use MLA formatting and referencing. Check out Purdue's Online Writing Lab (OWL) for the full list of how this works.

You can input your references manually and use Purdue's Online Writing Lab (OWL) or WorldCat.org to help you with the citation style and necessary information.
Alternatively, you can use a programme such as EndNote, EasyBib, Zotero or Mendeley, which are available online or as an add-on to your writing software. Word, Docs and Pages all have their own in-built versions, too.

REMEMBER
Foot notes are not included in your word count but should only be used for referencing or definitions. Any information that is worthy of being in your essay must be part of the body.

DRAFTING, EDITING AND FORMATTING

At what stage of the writing process would you do each of these things?

Once you have written and submitted your first draft, you will receive feedback from your supervisor to inform your changes from your final draft.

Your supervisor is only allowed to see and comment on one full draft but the writing is a process and you may need to revise and edit yourself a number of times before you are happy with the end result.

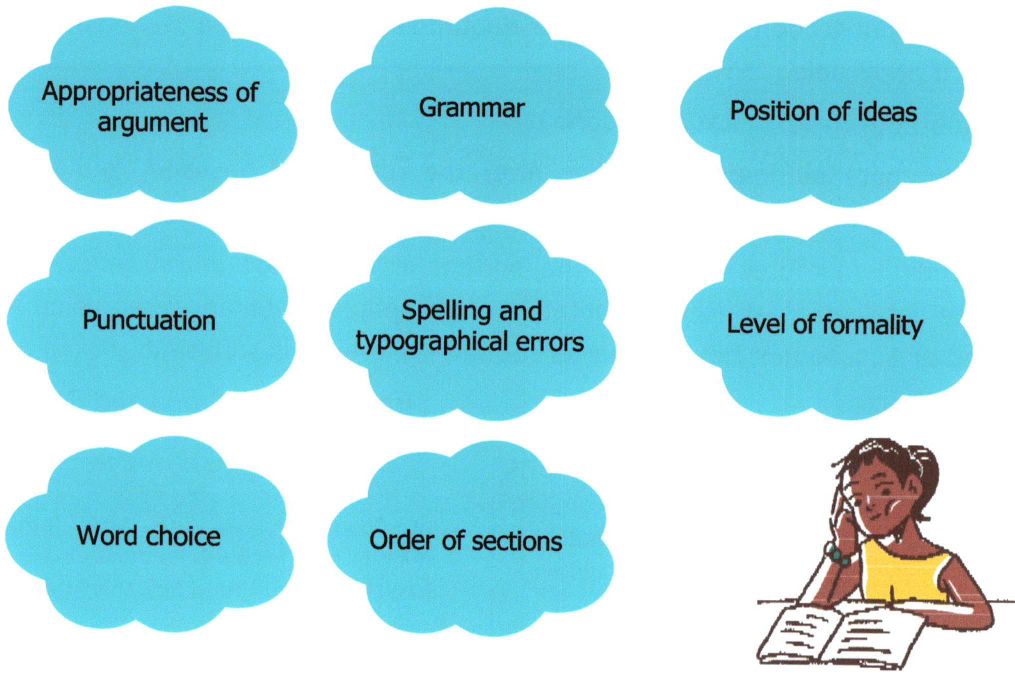

Criterion D

- Consistent presentation
- Clearly labelled diagrams and images
- Subheadings and labels
- Format and layout

Whole essay

- Cover page with essay title, research question, subject (and category) and word count
- DO NOT include your name on the document; if you want an identifier, use your candidate code (abc123)
- Number each page
- Label diagrams and images
- Subheadings appropriately formatted
- Correct referencing
- Include a list of works cited
- Size 10-12 font, Times New Roman or similar
- 1.5 or double spaced

DRAFTING, EDITING AND FORMATTING

Use the following questions to help you check through your work.

This is not an exhaustive list and does not have to be done in order.

- Am I still clear what my purposes were in this assignment? Is my topic clearly stated?
- Is there a clear central argument or point of view in the assignment? Do I feel I have achieved the assignment aim or purpose?
- Could I sum up my central position or point of view in the assignment in a sentence or two?
- Have I really answered the question/engaged with the set task? Is it clear what main points I am expressing in each paragraph? Have all sources of material been cited and referenced?
- Have I used examples when appropriate? Are my facts correct and up to date?
- Is there evidence of wide reading in this assignment?
- Are any quotations I have used relevant and correctly referenced? Have I made clear which points were not my own?
- Have I avoided bias and admitted alternative views? Do my conclusions follow logically from my evidence?
- Have I followed expected conventions in terms of referencing, bibliography, etc.? Will the structure of my essay be clear to the reader?
- Have I defined any key terms in the introduction?
- Have I made explicit connections between your introduction and conclusion? Do I make links between one paragraph or section and the next?
- Does each paragraph contain just one idea?
- Have I used headings where these might help the reader, e.g. in a report, or non- traditional essay?
- Have I used graphs, tables & diagrams where appropriate?
- Have I checked for obvious mistakes in spelling, punctuation and grammar?
- Does the language express my arguments with appropriate force and conviction? Is the document written in an appropriate style, e.g. in the third-person; objective language?
- Is the length and number of sentences in each paragraph suitably varied?
- Have you expressed your argument in a language which is clear and concise?
- Does the essay read smoothly and easily? (If in doubt, try reading it aloud.)

IB Extended Essay Layout

Title page – should include the title, research question (e.g. "How did phenomenon A cause phenomenon B?"), subject it is registered in, category (for language essays), essay theme and if it is a world studies essay, also state the theme and the two subjects utilized), total word count.

Contents page – should be at the beginning listing headings and subheadings along with corresponding page numbers these can be found on (all pages should be numbered). It is strongly recommended to insert the 'Automated Table of Contents'.

Introduction – should describe the focus and scope of this research, used sources, line of argument to be presented. As per the EE website, "The introduction should tell the reader what to expect in the essay. The introduction should make clear to the reader the focus of the essay, the scope of the research, in particular an indication of the sources to be used, and an insight into the line of argument to be taken"

A methodology section or other sections might also be appropriate. Also, there might be an Appendices section if you have supplementary material to add (this is not included in the total word count). Also note that starting with May 2018 session, abstract is **NOT** needed – adding it will unnecessarily steal roughly 300 words from the total word count, which will almost certainly prove detrimental (so it's wise to skip it).

The body – this is the main section where research, analysis, discussion, and evaluation is being performed. The structure might vary from subject to subject but it is essential that evidence and argument development is presented clearly and in appropriate order.

The Conclusion – says what has been achieved, including notes of any limitations and any questions that have not been resolved. While students might draw conclusions throughout the essay based on their findings, it is important that there is a final, summative conclusion at the end. This conclusion(s) must relate to the research question posed".

References and bibliography – students should adhere to a chosen academic citation style and use it consistently (different citations styles might be required depending on the discipline). Only those sources used in the body of the essay need to appear in the bibliography at the end.

Extended Essay student Agreement

Preparation:

- I met with my mentor and will keep him/her informed of my progress.
- I reviewed essay and subject area criteria in the IB Extended Essay Guide (available on the IB)
- I reviewed the extended essay format, assessment and grading criteria (available on the IB)
- I reviewed examples of research questions in the IB Extended Essay Guide and sample essays available in school.

Investigation and Citations:

- I gathered relevant information from a diverse range of sources (please consult CHS library's Extended Essay Research Guide on the Destiny homepage).
- I located primary sources, illustrations, graphs, and charts for my appendix (please consult CHS library's Extended Essay Research Guide on the Destiny homepage).
- I stored my sources in database folders, NoodleTools, or cited them on notecards.
- I used the citation style appropriate for my subject area in a consistent manner.
- I cited all facts, direct quotes and paraphrased ideas gathered from my sources (*including web pages), within my paper and in bibliography.

Argument and Conclusion:

- My research question is clearly and precisely stated in the introduction and is sharply focused so as to be effectively treated within the word limit.
- I support my argument with evidence that I have found through investigation, and all quotations are used as evidence to support my argument.
- I addressed and analyzed my research question by the conclusion of my essay.
- The pagination in my table of contents is correct.
- I reviewed my final draft to ensure that my essay...
    - does not exceed 4000 words;
    - has an abstract, introduction, conclusion and, if appropriate, appendix.
    - has proper pagination.
    - is well-written and has been spell-checked.
    - is incredibly *awesome*!

Quick checklist for your writing

QUESTION	Y/N
1. Have I answered the question yet?	
2. Have I made a case for a clearly stated conclusion?	
3. Have I used evidence, quotation and argument to make my case?	
4. Have I considered and answered possible counterarguments?	
5. Is the structure of my essay clearly signposted throughout?	
6. Have I acknowledged the sources of any quotations I've used?	
7. Have I provided a bibliography in the appropriate form?	
8. Is the tone of my essay appropriate for an academic context?	
9. Have I resorted to cliches or colloquialisms?	
10. Are there any adjectives or adverbs that I could remove?	
11. Is every paragraph relevant to the main argument of the essay?	
12. Have I made any slips in my use of apostrophes, commas or quotation marks?	
13. Have I spelt names of authors, places, books etc. correctly?	

Self Check: Evaluating your writing for critical thinking

Self Evaluation	Yes / No	Action
1. I am clear on my position on this subject and the reasons for my point of view.		Write your position down as a statement in one or two sentences. If you cannot do so, this suggests that your position isn't yet clear in your own mind. If possible, also check whether your point of view is clear to a friend or colleague who knows little about the subject.
2. My conclusion and/or recommendations are clear, based on the evidence, and written in tentative language where appropriate.		Write your conclusions first. Read these aloud; check that they make sense. Imagine someone tells you that your conclusion is wrong. What reasons would you give to defend it? Have you included all these reasons in your writing?
3. The material included is the most relevant to the subject.		Double-check that your line of reasoning meets the EE requirements. Does it match the statement you wrote about your position?
4. All sections of the assignment or report are relevant to the exact specifications of the task.		Read through each section or paragraph in turn, checking how the information contributes to your line of reasoning, leading to your conclusion or recommendations. Check that each answers your RQ.
5. I have analysed the structure of my argument. Reasons are presented in the best order and lead clearly towards the conclusion.		If not, write the reasons out in brief and consider how each is linked to the conclusion. Check whether the argument 'hops' from one point to another. Cluster similar reasons together and indicate how each contributes to the main argument or conclusion.
6. The argument stands out clearly from other information. I have selected the best examples.		Check you have not presented so much detail that the main argument is lost. An analysis of few examples or details is better than a superficial approach to lots of material. Select carefully.
7. My reasons are clearly linked to one another and to the conclusion(s).		Check that each paragraph opens with a clear link to what has gone before or signals a change in the direction of your argument using 'signal words.'
8. My main reasons and key points stand out clearly to the reader.		Take a marker pen and highlight the sentence that sums up the main point or reason covered in each paragraph. If you find this difficult, it is likely that your reader will find it hard to identify your points. If large sections of a paragraph are highlighted, then it is probable that you haven't summarized its main point sufficiently.

Self Evaluation	Yes / No	Action
9. My facts are accurate.		Don't rely on opinion or memory. Check that your sources are reputable and up to date. Investigate whether anything published more recently gives different information. Check that you have reported the facts accurately, and without distortion.
10. I have included reference to relevant theories.		Find out the schools of thought or theories related to this subject. Make a critical evaluation of these to identify where they support of conflict with your argument.
11. I make use of other people's research as supporting evidence to strengthen my argument.		Check what has been written or produced on this subject by other people. Include references to relevant items that best support your point of view.
12. I have cited the source of information for evidence and theories to which I refer.		Write out the details of the references in brief within the text, and in full at the end of the writing.
13. I included a reasoned evaluation of views that do not support my own argument.		Find out what has been written that contradicts your point of view and consider any other potential objections that could be raised. Evaluate these as part of your line of reasoning. Make it clear why your reasons are more convincing than opposing points of view. Identify any flaws, gaps or inconsistencies in the counter arguments.
14. My writing is mainly analytical and contains only brief, essential descriptive writing.		Check whether all sections of descriptive writing and background information are essential to understanding your reasoning or are part of the conventions of the type of report you are writing. Keep descriptions very brief, look for ways of summarizing them and link them clearly to your main argument. Beware of wordy introductions.
15. I have checked my argument for inconsistencies.		Check whether any of the reasons or evidence you have used could be interpreted as contradicting what you have written elsewhere in the piece of writing.
16. I have given clear indications of levels of probability or uncertainty.		Check that your writing indicates your judgement of how likely it is that the conclusion is accurate and irrefutable. If there is a chance that research findings could be interpreted differently by someone else, use appropriate language to indicate a level of uncertainty or ambiguity.
17. My current beliefs are not unfairly distorting my argument.		If any section of your EE covers a subject where you have strong beliefs or interests, be especially careful that you have checked the evidence supports your reasoning. It is important that your arguments come across as calm and reasoned in a way that will convince your reader. Check several times and be careful not to include emotive language or poorly substantiated opinions.
18. I have covered all the required aspects of the assignment.		Check the [EE] details carefully. Tick aspects already completed so it is clear what else you must do.

Final draft of the Extended Essay –Checklist

Students should consider and complete the following checklist prior to handing in their first and final submission of the Extended Essay to their Supervisor.

This is created for Business Management EE that can be adapted to any other subject.

Criterion A – Focus and method (6 marks)			
This assessment criterion focuses on the **topic**, the **research question**, and the **methodology**. It assesses the explanation of the focus of the research (this includes the topic and the research question), how the research will be undertaken, and how the **focus** is maintained throughout the essay.			
	Yes	No	Needs work
The topic is clearly stated (which is not phrased as a question).			
The research question is phrased as an actual question.			
The research question is sharply focused so can be addressed within the 4,000-word count limit.			
The research question focuses on a real business problem or issue that is worthy of investigation.			
The research question provides opportunities for intellectual discovery and creativity/originality.			
There is an explanation of how the research is helpful (adds value) in addressing the topic and research question.			
The research question can be addressed by the use of secondary resources in the first instance.			
If primary sources have been used, it is because the research provides information that is not accessible from secondary sources.			
Primary research, if used, significantly enhances the value of the secondary data presented in the essay.			
There is a focus on the research question throughout the essay.			
Research findings and arguments are causally linked to the research question throughout the essay.			
The methodologies and research sources identified in the introduction have been used in the essay.			
Each and every paragraph is directly related to the research question.			
There are no superfluous materials included in any part of the essay.			

Criterion B – Knowledge and understanding (6 marks)			
This assessment criterion examines the extent to which the research relates to the subject area/discipline used to explore the research question, and the way in which this **knowledge and understanding** is demonstrated through the use of appropriate **terminology and concepts**.			
	Yes	No	Needs work
Relevant subject-specific terminology, tools, techniques, and concepts are defined and/or explained, in the context of the research question.			
Subject-specific terminology, tools, and techniques are used in a consistent and appropriate way throughout the essay to address the research question.			
Sources of data and information have been clearly identified.			
The data and information included in the essay are of direct relevance to the research question.			
The data selected offers appropriate breadth and depth in addressing the research question. Possible sources include: • company data and annual reports • news media articles • academic journals • magazine articles • industry analyses • business management textbooks • general business management books • encyclopedias.			
Appropriate business management tools, theories, and techniques have been integrated effectively throughout the essay (theory has not been presented as a separate section in the essay).			
All sources have been accurately recorded in the bibliography.			

Criterion C – Critical thinking (12 marks)			
This assessment criterion examines the extent to which critical thinking skills have been used to **analyse** and **evaluate** the **research** undertaken.			
	Yes	**No**	**Needs work**
The research question is a probing one.			
The relevance of the chosen tools, techniques, and theories (to the research question) has been explained, i.e. how the tools, techniques, and theories help to answer the research question.			
There is evidence of engagement with secondary sources that are used in a critical and reflective way.			
There is clear evidence of critical thinking skills when analysing research sources and information presented in the essay.			
Business management tools, techniques, and theories have been evaluated, as necessary.			
Alternative viewpoints are acknowledged in order to critically evaluate arguments and conclusions presented in the essay.			
There is acknowledgement of the quality, balance, and quantity of the research sources.			
Any personal views are questioned in light of the research conducted by considering opposing perspectives of others.			
Where appropriate to the research question, both quantitative and qualitative research has been included.			
Discussions are explicitly and directly linked to the research question and the secondary data sources that have been cited.			
There is inclusion of research materials and/or tools, theories, and techniques that go beyond the IB Business Management syllabus.			
There is acknowledgement of the limitations and weaknesses of the methodology and data sources used in the research.			
Appropriate analytical tools from the business management syllabus have been included, such as: • Ansoff Matrix • Boston Consultancy Group Matrix • Break-even analysis • Decision trees • Financial statements and ratio analysis • Fishbone diagram • Force field analysis • Position (perception) maps • Stakeholder analysis • STEEPLE analysis • SWOT analysis			

Criterion C – Critical thinking (12 marks)			
This assessment criterion examines the extent to which critical thinking skills have been used to **analyse** and **evaluate** the **research** undertaken.			
	Yes	No	Needs work
The essay is written in an objective way, without personal biases or preconceptions.			
The essay is evidently analytical and evaluative rather than descriptive.			
The research results and findings have been used effectively to analyse the research question.			
There is clear research evidence to back up the analysis and evaluation in the body of the essay.			
Judgements are made and these have been fully substantiated, i.e. they are consistent with the argument presented in the essay and supported by evidence.			
The research question as stated on the title page and in the introduction are directly addressed in the conclusion of the essay.			
There is a culminating conclusion that summarizes all of the research and responses in relation to the research question.			
The conclusion(s) has (have) been derived from the previous discussions in the body of the essay.			
The conclusion(s) is (are) consistent with the findings, discussions, and arguments presented in the body of the essay.			
There are no new ideas included in the conclusion(s), except for unanswered questions (where appropriate).			
The conclusion(s) directly refers to and answers the research question.			
The conclusion(s) has (have) been justified and validated, and derived from the evidence researched.			
The conclusion does **not** include any recommendations (as they are not required in the essay).			
Where appropriate, the conclusion indicates any unresolved questions, or new questions that have arisen from the study.			

Criterion D – Formal presentation (4 marks)			
This assessment criterion examines the extent to which the **presentation** follows the standard format expected for academic writing and the extent to which this aids effective **communication**.			
	Yes	No	Needs work
A title page is included, showing the: • Topic • Research question • Session number (e.g. May 2022), and • Personal code (e.g. gmh007).			
The candidate's name and number do **not** appear on any of the pages of the essay, including the title page.			
A contents page has been included, and contains the following: • Introduction • Methodology • Main body, including appropriate sub-headings • Conclusion • Bibliography • Appendices • Numbered pages			
The essay is formatted as follows, using: • Arial or Times New Roman font • Font size 11 or 12 • 1.5 or double-spaced • Numbered pages.			
There is a clear, consistent, and acceptable format used to write the essay.			
There is effective and appropriate use of diagrams and graphs, where relevant to the research question.			
Diagrams, graphs, charts, and/or tables, if used, are digitally produced.			
The bibliography is accurate and complete, encompassing all works cited in the essay.			
The bibliography and references follow a consistent format.			
The appendices, if included, contain relevant supplementary evidence/material.			
Any items placed in the appendices are relevant and have been referenced and/or referred to in the essay.			
The appendices, if included, have been page numbered.			

Criterion D – Formal presentation (4 marks)			
	Yes	No	Needs work
Each appendix item appears on a separate page with an appropriate title. These are clearly listed in the Contents page, with correct page numbering.			
References (and in-text citation, if used) appear throughout the essay, including appropriate page numbering.			
The ideas and arguments are written in a clear and structured manner.			
The essay is saved as an acceptable file type (for electronic upload on IBIS): • PDF • DOC • DOCX • RTF			
The file size must not exceed 10MB.			
It is easy to follow the structure of the essay.			
Headings (and sub-headings if used) do not distract from the overall structure of the essay or argument presented.			
The written report is within the word count limit of **4,000** words.			

Criterion E – Engagement (6 marks)			
This assessment criterion examines the student's **engagement** with their research focus and the research process. It will be applied by the examiner at the end of the assessment of the essay and is based solely on the candidate's reflections as detailed on the RPPF document, with the supervisory comments and extended essay itself providing the context for this. Only the first **500 words** are read and assessed.			
	Yes	No	Needs work
The reflections highlight your thinking, planning, and reviewing at **three** distinct stages during the EE process.			
There is reflective thinking about the approach to the written report and its limitations.			
There is mention of at least one adjustment/change made to the research as the essay progressed.			
There is clear evidence of reflective, critical thinking in the essay, thereby demonstrating engagement with the process.			
There is justified consideration of at least one thing that you would have done differently if you were to write the essay again.			
There is evidence of reflection on any biases or limitations that may have weakened the strength of the research or affected the objectivity of the findings.			
The RPPF document has been completed within the 500-word count limit.			
A declaration of the time spent with the EE supervisor has been declared on the RPPF (3 to 5 hours).			
The RPPF document is duly signed by both the candidate and the supervisor.			

Are you ready for these viva voce questions?

Here some examples of what might be asked at your viva voce. Before the meeting it is advised you think about these questions and themes. Be proactive and engaged in the process by being able to elaborate on your thoughts.

Focus:

- Celebration of the completion of the essay
- Outcome of the process
- What skills have been learnt? In terms of research and process

1. To what extend were your initial ideas realized?
2. Were your original plans/ideas realistic and appropriate?
3. What do you think your Successes were in this process?
4. What were most rewarding aspects of the entire process?
5. How will this experience prepare you for future work of this Nature (in college or employment?)

Source: IB Teacher Support Material.

A. What conclusions did You arrive at during the research and writing of your EE?

B. What would you consider to be the most (and Least) rewarding aspect of your research and writing process?

C. What figures or illustrations did you include? Why did you choose those?

D. What source contradicted the general ideas of your research? In what way specifically did the source contradict them? Did you include it? Why? Why? not?

E. Which of your sources did you find to be the most helpful? Why?

F. Select a few- sections from the Work and ask the student questions pertain mg to their meaning. why they were used and their relevance (for example. Why did you select this source to support your points or what do you think X was getting at when he said Y?

G. What have you learned about your topic from researching and writing about it?

H. What challenges did you encounter when researching aid writing the EE? How did you go about overcoming them?

I. What unanswered question are you Left with?

J. How successful do you believe you've been with regard to the answering your RO?

K. Is there anything that contributed to the EE that is not immediately evident in the essay itself? (such as museum visits and email exchanges with participants, scientists and authors?

Source: Lekanides, Kosta. Extended Essay. Course Companion, Oxford OUP, 2016. Print.

I. If you were to do this research again, what would you do differently and why?

II. Were there any surprises in your learning journey? What did you learn from this?

III. What does success mean to you in the process of producing your EE?

IV. To what extent do you think you have been successful in this process?

V. Were the strategies you used for your research question the most appropriate for achieving success?

VI. If you used alternative research methodologies and/or subject-specific theories. would this have led to a different outcome?

VII. Are there any new or unanswered questions that emerged as a result of your research?

VIII. What advice would you give to next year's students who have yet to write their EE?

Source: Hoang, Paul & Taylor, Chris. Extended Essay: Skills for Success, London: Hodder Education. 2017. Print.

Supervisor Marking EE Criteria/Rubric (Final Draft)

This front page is a summary sheet for details and feedback. Please adapt and edit to your judgement.

STUDENT	SUPERVISOR	DATE

FEEDBACK FOR CRITERION A: FOCUS AND METHOD
FEEDBACK FOR CRITERION B: KNOWLEDGE AND UNDERSTANDING
FEEDBACK FOR CRITERION C: CRITICAL THINKING
FEEDBACK FOR PRESENTATION

ESTIMATED SCORE (PLEASE CIRCLE)				
E	D	C	B	A

TIMELINE 2024-2026

DATE	PHASE	DETAILS
12.01.XX	Intro to the EE	What is the EE? • Understand requirements and begin generating ideas for topics
26.01.XX	Creating questions & using the researcher's reflection space	• More detailed lines of inquiry & what makes an effective Research Question • What the Rearcher's Reflection Space is and how to utilise it.
23.02.XX	Initial research and referencing skills	• How to find and article • How to read and article • Citing and referencing • Create and annotated bibliography Between now and next session, start researching
16.03.XX	Subject specific requirements & choosing a question	Working on bibliographies • What have you discovered? • What do you want to say? Sample EEs
25.03.XX	Submit proposal	Complete proposal with suggested topic, subject, question and sources so far. From this, supervisors will be assigned. Over the break, continue your research.
11-22.04.XX	First meeting with supervisor and first mandatory reflection	• Meet with supervisor to discuss initial ideas. Take your annotated bibliography and proposal. • Complete your first mandatory reflection on the RPPF
20.04 and 04.05.XX	Peer Presentations and reflections	• Review where you are in the process and what you have found • Prepare and present to the class this research • Decide your next steps
18.05.XX	Exemplars, outlines and effective analysis	During this time, meet with your supervisor as • Read and grade and example EE in your subject • Create a checklist of criteria for success • Create and outline for your essay and submit to supervisors by 01.06.22 During this time, meet with your supervisor as necessary and continue and further research

<table>
<tr><th>DATE</th><th>PHASE</th><th>DETAILS</th></tr>
<tr><td>01.06.XX</td><td>Analysis and Drafting</td><td>• Understand the drafting process and work on your first draft
• Peer review outlines
• Explore and write a sample analysis, focusing on Criterion C
During this time, meet with your supervisor as necessary and complete any further research. Submit your introduction and first analytical paragraph/section to your supervisor by 20.06.22</td></tr>
<tr><td>22.06.XX</td><td>Referencing</td><td>• Types of referencing
• Creating a reference and bibliography, including reference management software
• Formatting of the EE</td></tr>
<tr><td>Summer Work</td><td colspan="2">EE drafting – complete the first full draft. This will be due for submission 08.09.22. Submit a copy to the task on ManageBac and email a version to your supervisor, copying in Ms Kirsty</td></tr>
<tr><td>14.09.XX</td><td>Re-drafting and editing skills</td><td>• Getting and using feedback
• The redrafting process
• Recap of the requirements of RPPF</td></tr>
<tr><td>12-24.09.XX</td><td>Feedback and second RPPF</td><td>Meet with your supervisor for feedback on your first draft. Complete your second mandatory reflection on the RPPF. Between now and the final deadline, work on your final draft. Meet your supervisor as necessary and keep your Researcher's Reflection Space up to date.</td></tr>
<tr><td>12.10.XX</td><td>Review of analysis and essay clinic</td><td>• Recap and review any outstanding elements and criteria.
• Peer assess or bring a section to discuss as necessary.
Between now and the final deadline, work on your final draft. Meet your supervisor as necessary and keep your Researcher's Reflection Space up to date.</td></tr>
<tr><td>08.12.XX</td><td colspan="2">Final draft due. Submit a copy to the task on ManageBac and email a version to your supervisor, copying in Ms Kirsty.</td></tr>
<tr><td>10.01.XX</td><td rowspan="2">The Viva Voce</td><td>Explanation of the viva voce process and requirements.</td></tr>
<tr><td>10-13.01.XX</td><td>Meet with your supervisor to complete your viva voce interview and your final reflection.</td></tr>
</table>

Examples of Research Topics

Biology extended essay topics

1. Endosymbiotic theory – evidence for how ancient bacteria were "subjugated" and transformed into eukaryotic cell organelles (mitochondria, chloroplasts)
2. Fungi – metabolic and molecular similarities with both plants and animals
3. Evaluate supporting life evolution on Earth near hydrothermal vents on the ocean floor
4. How millennia of breeding made domesticated dogs respond to eye contact by bonding (by producing oxytocin hormone)
5. Biological mechanisms of magnetoreception for geographical navigation in various organisms
6. Benefits and advances in modelling entire organisms in silico (using computers) – the example of Mycoplasma genitalium as a "whole cell" model
7. An analysis of recent adaptive traits evolved in humans (tolerance to arsenic in drinking water in Patagonia, better nutrient assimilation from dairy products in Europe, or from vegetal food in Africa, etc.)
8. Neanderthalian DNA in people with European ancestry

Psychology extended essay topics

1. An interpretation of various historic personalities using the Maslow's hierarchy of needs theory
2. Abuse suffered in childhood as a reason for oppressive behavior in adulthood
3. Instability of memories – how replaying a memory can alter it. Implanting false memories.
4. Novel methods to treat phobias
5. Self-help therapies using cognitive behavioral therapy
6. Lucid dreaming – proven techniques to take control over your dreams
7. Imaginative character and trauma as prerequisites for multiple personality disorder onset
8. Importance of spaced repetition in learning and modern productivity tools

English extended essay topics

1. An analysis of neologisms (new words) in modern English – the main sources/fields of knowledge or life they come from
2. How English grammar rules, word order, etc. influence the way we think (there could be links with psychology)
3. Tracing naturalized English words with origin in Sanskrit language
4. Systematizing differences between American English and British English

5. Most popular English words assimilated by other cultures during British colonialism
6. French influences on English language evolution
7. American English phonetics – general distinctive patterns systematized
8. Foreign languages from which English borrowed words ranked by contribution
9. English learning curve as compared to other languages (in categories like pronunciation, grammar, spelling and various subcategories (e.g. article use, verb tense, etc.)
10. Main semantic categories in which borrowed Spanish words fall into among English speaking Americans

Literature extended essay topics

1. Gabriel Garcia Marquez's writing style (distinctive features, innovation, etc.)
2. Postmodernist elements in Kurt Vonnegut's Slaughterhouse Five
3. Artificial languages in literature (basic statistics, features, limitations, most comprehensive examples, etc.)
4. Role of supernatural in Macbeth
5. Evolution of ideal woman portrayal in literature
6. Major stylistic Innovations brought by various Nobel prize winners in literature
7. A depiction of human nature in Kafka's Metamorphosis

Geography extended essay topics

1. Role of geological evidence in inspiring Darwin's theory on the origin of species
2. Extensive coral bleaching across the Great Barrier Reef resulting from climate change
3. Response of the Caribbean ecosystem following the Deepwater Horizon oil spill
4. Salt accumulation in soil resulting from unsustainable irrigation practices
5. Anticipated climate change impact on oceanic currents
6. Massive power outages caused by solar storms – future prevention strategies
7. Massive eruption of the Vesuvius supervolcano as the potential cause of Neanderthal extinction
8. Polar vortex instability resulting from climate change
9. Siberian permafrost thawing – current estimates of methane volume risking to be released and potential implications (according to models)
10. Impact of fertilizers on the ecosystem of the Mississippi river

History extended essay topics

1. Discovery of the Rosetta stone – event history and importance
2. Oldest human settlements as suggested by archeological data, radioactive dating, etc.
3. Property rights of black people during the Reconstruction period following the Civil War
4. Use of corruption and deception by Abraham Lincoln to pass the 13th
5. Estimates of casualties due to epidemics following landing of Spanish colonizers
7. Roosevelt's evolving rhetoric in WW2 regarding involvement in WW2 against Nazis
8. Simultaneous invasion of Poland by Nazi Germany and USSR in 1939
9. The two-millennial history behind the Terracotta Army: what does it tell us about the Chinese society back then
10. The use of human-piloted torpedoes by the Imperial Japanese Navy in WW2

Physics extended essay topics

1. "Spooky action at a distance": quantum entanglement – experimental evidence of a most mysterious phenomenon in universe
2. Recreating nuclear reactions happening in the Sun back on Earth: an international scientific quest of harnessing unlimited energy from nuclear fusion reactions (to focus on stellarators and tokamaks)
3. The amazing physics of Prince Ruppert's drops
4. Physical mechanisms underlying Earth's magnetic field
5. Cosmic microwave background as evidence supporting the Big Bang
6. Redshifted light from galaxies as evidence supporting an expanding universe
7. Gravitational waves - generation, propagation laws, detection on Earth, etc.
8. A revolution in imaging space: telescope arrays – how do they work?
9. Physical properties of laminar flow – application in biosecurity (e.g. ventilation hoods), engineering, decoration (e.g. creative fountains), etc.
10. Physical explanation of flashing lights preceding some earthquakes

Film extended essay topics

1. Correlation between IMDB marks and various national and international film
2. Filming techniques used by Guy Ritchie
3. Metamorphosis of masculinity in modern times as depicted in Fight club
4. Varieties of timeline manipulation techniques in cinematography
6 Massively distorted scientist or scientific method portrayal in Sci-Fi movies
5. Moving camera – innovative techniques (e.g. as used in Matrix, or Guy Ritchie's movie)

6. Computer graphics capabilities and use in modern cinematography
7. Avoiding the "soap opera" effect - why movies stay at 24 frames per second (including future predictions)

Economics extended essay topics

1. NAFTA's impact on Mexican corn producers
2. Correlation strength between functional democratic institutions and economic wealth worldwide (including mechanisms)
3. Strategies used and advantages exploited by modern China to propel its economy
4. Offshore financial centers as a major cause of global economic obscurity – measures to impose global transparency
5. How to handle taxation in a world dominated by global corporations
6. World's largest corporations as classified by country
7. Impact aging population on global economics
8. South Korean phenomenon – reasons for economic miracle
9. Implications of the recent discovery of huge rare metal deposits by Japan
10. Anticipated economic effects following from job substitution by AI in the USA

World studies extended essays topics

1. Common elements shared by world religions (e.g. birth from a virgin, resurrection, antagonism between evil and good, life after death)
2. Universe formation (cosmogony) myths in various religions
3. Heaven and hell in Christian thought
4. Depiction of life after death in various religions (similarities, differences)
5. Missionary behavior/attitude as a prerequisite for active expansion of a religion
6. A comparison of attitudes adopted by Buddhism and Christianity towards scientific progress/ discoveries
7. Good vs bad (pure vs sinful) – human nature in various religions
8. Jesus Christ's figure in Islam and Judaism

MEETING NOTES

DATE	ITEMS DISCUSSED	TO DO

DATE	ITEMS DISCUSSED	TO DO

DATE	ITEMS DISCUSSED	TO DO

DATE	ITEMS DISCUSSED	TO DO

DATE	ITEMS DISCUSSED	TO DO

Recommendations for the supervision of students

- First and foremost, supervisors and students should familiarize themselves extensively with the Extended essay guide, as this remains the most crucial place to fully understand the different components and aspects of the EE.
- Students need to be guided and supported while undertaking this research project. Although some skills can be taught throughout the Diploma programme also by subject teachers, there are a number of elements where students need to rely on the support of their supervisor.
- Some of the most important ones include:
    - **Constructing the research question**. The entire EE depends on the appropriateness of the research question. Supervisors need to give practical and constructive guidance to students in order to construct appropriate research questions.
    - **Assisting with secondary sources**. Supervisors need to help students develop a critical approach towards appropriate and inappropriate secondary sources to use. Simply putting questions in online search engines and using the proposed sources there, is not enough and will not allow for in-depth analysis.
    - **Instructing on how to carry out appropriate referencing and bibliography**. Especially the former is important to avoid issues of malpractice and make sure that students are not plagiarizing work by researchers.
- ***The increased use of artificial intelligence (AI), if applied by students in their EE, needs to be done appropriately and be acknowledged within the EE. Although this is still a tool that is in development, students need to be aware that over-reliance on AI tools for writing can be detected by examiners.***
- Additionally, although students are allowed to choose any subject for their EE, **it is advisable for them to choose an EE in a subject they are taking as part of their Diploma programme,** as this will provide a good amount of contextual and analytical knowledge.
- If choosing a subject outside of their Diploma programme, students need to make sure that they fill this gap in knowledge.
- Finally, the IB cannot answer queries on topic suitability, but only help with guidance on better understanding the Extended essay guide and category classification. The choice of topic and the value of the sources used, remains with students and supervisors.

References

English Language Teaching Centre, 2014. *Academic Essay Writing for Postgraduates: Independent Study Version*. Edinburgh: Edinburgh University

International Baccalaureate Organization, 2014. *Effective Citing and Referencing*. Cardiff: International Baccalaureate Organization.

International Baccalaureate Organization, 2016 (2022). *Extended Essay Guide.* Cardiff: International Baccalaureate Organization

International Baccalaureate Organization, 2016. *International Baccalaureate Diploma Programme Subject Brief, Diploma Programme Core: Extended essay, including the world studies option.* Cardiff: International Baccalaureate Organization

Lekanides, K, 2016. *Extended Essay: Course Companion*. Oxford: Oxford University Press.

Navas, A, 2021. *Mrs Metacognition Student Research Journal.* USA: Alison Navas.

Philpot, B, 2021. *Extended Essay Support Site* from https://philpot.education/mod/page/view.php?id=443. [Accessed 24 June 2022] Amsterdam: Philpot Education B.V.

SAGE, 2022. *Doing Your Education Research Project* from https://uk.sagepub.com/en- gb/eur/doing-your-education-research-project. [Accessed 24 June 2022] London: SAGE Publications

https://resources.ibo.org/dp/subject-group/Extended-essay-first-assessment-2018/topic/Subject-reports/resource/11162-431039/?

www.ingramcontent.com/pod-product-compliance
Ingram Content Group UK Ltd.
Pitfield, Milton Keynes, MK11 3LW, UK
UKHW060107300726
14090UKWH00003B/393

* 9 7 9 8 8 9 6 9 9 4 9 0 9 *